THE WARE MUTINY 1647

Order Restored or
Revolution Defeated?

Alan Thomson

THE WARE MUTINY 1647

Order Restored or Revolution Defeated?

Published by
The Rockingham Press
in association with
The Ware Museum Trust

Published in 1996
by
The Rockingham Press
11 Musley Lane,
Ware, Herts
SG12 7EN

British Library Cataloguing-in-Publication Data

A catalogue record for this book
is available from the British Library

ISBN 1 873468 39 3

Printed in Great Britain
by Biddles Limited,
Guildford

For my wife
who had to re-live the mutiny
a number of times

Acknowledgements

This book could not have been produced without the help of many people. In particular, I would like to thank the staff of a number of archives, libraries and record offices, and David Perman for his support, advice and encouragement.

I would also like to thank the Marc Fitch Fund and the Isobel Thornley Bequest for their generous grants, which have made it possible for the book to be published at a price within the budgets of students.

The sources of photographs and other illustrations are given in the captions, but special thanks must be given here to John Goldsmith, Museums Officer for Cambridgeshire and Curator of the Cromwell Museum in Huntingdon, and to Melanie Bunch of the Royal Armouries.

One of many paintings of Oliver Cromwell by Robert Walker. This one was painted for his daughter, Bridget, who was married to Henry Ireton. (Cromwell Museum, Huntingdon)

Contents

Illustrations and plans

Plans

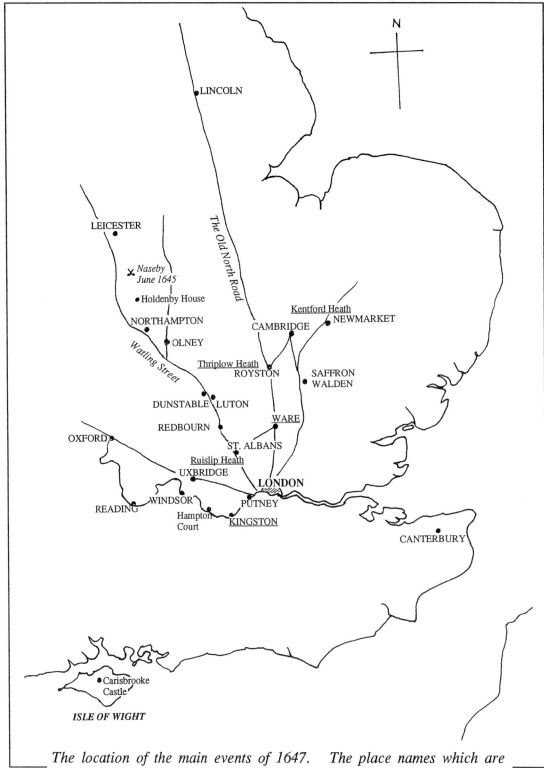

The location of the main events of 1647. The place names which are underlined are those of the various rendezvous of the New Model Army.

1
Introduction:
"these seditious irregularities"

On Monday 15th November 1647, Private Richard Arnold of Colonel Robert Lilburne's foot regiment of the New Model Army was shot by two of his fellow soldiers, after a court-martial in Corkbush Field [1] between Hertford and Ware. They had all three been found guilty of mutiny and forced to draw lots to see who would shoot the loser. Arnold lost. The commander-in-chief of the army who ordered the sentence was General Sir Thomas Fairfax. Also present in the field were his Lieutenant-General Oliver Cromwell, M.P. for Cambridge, and Commissary-General Henry Ireton — in other words, the second and third-in-command. These events and others that took place on the same day between Hertford and Ware nearly 350 years ago were referred to at the time by Parliament as "these seditious irregularities." They have also caused considerable controversy amongst historians since then, one even questioning whether a mutiny took place at all. A key issue that is still debated is: did these events merely see a restoration of order within the army, or was a radical revolution from below defeated?

This book is designed to put together the various pieces of evidence to: — identify the groups which contributed to the political chaos that followed the defeat of the King in 1646 and to the defeat of the mutineers in 1647; — explain why the King, Parliament and the army failed to come to a constitutional agreement in 1647 and why the mutineers' proposals were unacceptable to them; — recreate the events that took place on the 15th November; — analyse the various interpretations that have been put on these events; — and attempt to answer a few of the unanswered questions relating to them and suggest why the Ware Mutiny was and remains a significant episode in English history.

---

[1] *In some sources, the original spelling is Cockbush. Modern historians favour Corkbush, but this may be a mistranscription of an 'r' for a 'c', which look similar in some 17th century written hands. Although Corkbush Field was and is in Hertford, historians have always identified the mutiny as taking place at Ware, which was then economically more important than the neighbouring county town.*

The Ware Mutiny has a place both in the history of the English Revolution, which saw the execution of Charles I in 1649, and in that of Oliver Cromwell who became Lord Protector in 1653. It is seen as a turning point in the struggle for control of the parliamentary army between General Fairfax and the senior officers on the one hand and radical soldiers and junior officers and their "Leveller" allies on the other. The Levellers were a radical group based in London, who proposed a written constitution and the end of the monarchy and who had infiltrated the army during the summer of 1647. Their defeat at Corkbush Field, and later at Burford in 1649, signalled the end of attempts at radical political revolution. However their defeat also contributed to the rise of Oliver Cromwell, who effectively took over the command of the army from Fairfax, when it invaded Ireland in 1649 and Scotland in 1650. Those hostile to Cromwell — both at the time and since — have seen his actions at the Ware Mutiny as a deliberate move to assert his power and influence by defeating a threat from below, from those who had previously hoped that he would support their cause. However the evidence is not clear as to what role Cromwell actually played. Those who have sympathised with the Levellers have seen the suppression of the mutiny as a betrayal by Cromwell of all the army stood for, and as a deliberate move to prevent a democratic revolution. However the view that the Levellers were democratic in the modern sense is open to interpretation. Others have questioned whether an actual mutiny took place, or whether Corkbush Field was more the occasion for punishing those who had mutinied a few days earlier at St. Albans, Luton and Dunstable.

As 1997 sees the 350th anniversary of the Ware Mutiny, and 1999 the 400th anniversary of the birth of Cromwell, controversies surrounding both are likely to continue.

2
The Historical Background

The end of the First Civil War

The Civil War had started in the autumn of 1642. The key turning points included the Battle of Marston Moor, outside York, in 1644 — when the Scots intervened to help the parliamentary army defeat the royalists — and the decisive Battle at Naseby in Northamptonshire in June 1645. Cromwell played a prominent part as a leader of the cavalry in both these battles. Following up these victories, Fairfax defeated the royalists again at Langport in the south-west and laid siege to Bristol, which was stormed in September. In 1646, the parliamentary army moved through the south-west taking towns, castles and fortified houses. The last royalist field army surrendered in March and their headquarters at Oxford in June. The King however had escaped from Oxford in disguise, and passed through Hertfordshire on his way north to join the Scots, who he thought would treat him more leniently than the English. Following a deal with the Scots in December, the King was handed over to the English Parliament and lodged at Holdenby or Holmby Hall in Northampton-shire in February 1647.

The New Model Army

King Charles I had been defeated in 1646 by the parliamentary New Model Army, a new-modelled or reorganised army whose regiments had become virtually professional soldiers. It had been formed in 1645 from a number of existing armies controlled by different aristocratic or regional commanders. The success of Marston Moor had not been followed up and a quarrel had broken out between the Earl of Manchester, the commander of the Army of the Eastern Association, and his deputy, Cromwell. Their army drawn from East Anglia and the eastern counties, including Cambridge and Hertfordshire, had a reputation for having disciplined soldiers but allowing the spread of radical religion. Manchester, a conservative Presbyterian [2],

---

[2] *The term 'Presbyterian' has been used by many historians to denote not just a particular religious faction, but the more conservative or peace-party group within Parliament. However other historians are not agreed on the exact political labels that should be used about groups in the early 1640s.*

objected to Cromwell's policy of promoting radical young officers with unorthodox religious persuasions. Cromwell and other more radical M.P.s on the other hand wanted to remove the old aristocratic leadership from the parliamentary armies, because they regarded them as unwilling to pursue the war effectively and as hankering after a deal with the King before he had been defeated.

After the failure of the parliamentary army at the second battle of Newbury, two measures of reform had been pushed through Parliament. The first, the *Self-Denying Ordinance* effectively removed the aristocratic leadership from the army and the second set up the New Model Army. It was made up of reorganised regiments from

The army chaplain, Hugh Peter (Cromwell Museum, Huntingdon)

the Eastern Association and the former armies of General Waller and the Earl of Essex, as well as other provincial army units and latterly royalist deserters. Though this new army had rounded up the defeated royalists in the First Civil War, it was not disbanded and no political settlement had been reached by the summer of 1647, a year after the war had ended. This was largely because the King was able to play off one parliamentary faction against another and play on the fears of different religious and national groups. Many regiments had not been paid for months and were in dispute with Parliament over their arrears and rights. In 1646 there had been reports of mutinies or disturbances among the provincial forces in twenty-two English counties, and the main army had been used to help disband some of these forces but there were to be a further seventeen mutinies in the summer of 1647 (though, what are sometimes later referred to as 'mutinies', were in fact civilian disturbances).

A major influence on the army both during and after the war were the army chaplains appointed to each regiment. These men, like Hugh Peter, were reported as going into battle with a Bible in one hand and a pistol in the other. They led the troops in psalm-singing as they marched, encouraged soldiers to pray before battle and delivered fiery sermons about defeating the enemies of God in a righteous conflict. Not only were the chaplains essential for building morale but they were also agents of moral discipline. Cromwell had the reputation for enforcing harsh penalties against looters and appointing chaplains who would preach a godly message. A problem for the more conservative Presbyterians in Parliament was that these chaplains came to lead members of the sects — including radical Independents who saw their flock as an independent congregation or gathered church; Baptists who insisted that only adult baptism was appropriate; and more extreme orators preaching that the King was anti-Christ and that his defeat would fulfil biblical prophecy. It was this army, permeated by a variety of religious radicals, that the senior officers had to try and control in the face of political radicalisation by the Levellers.

The Grandees

The senior officers, referred to by their critics as the 'Grandees', who were present at Corkbush Field on the 15th November, were General Sir Thomas Fairfax, the commander-in-chief of all parliamentary forces, Lieutenant-General Oliver Cromwell, his second-in-command and the future Lord Protector, who had managed to retain his seat in the House of Commons as M.P. for Cambridge, and his third-in-Command, Commissary-General Henry Ireton. Ireton was M.P. for Appleby and had married Cromwell's daughter Bridget in the previous summer. General Sir Thomas Fairfax had replaced the Earl of Essex as overall commander of the army in 1645. Unlike Cromwell, Fairfax and Essex had both had some previous military experience fighting with the Dutch for the Protestant cause in the Thirty Years' War. Fairfax has been described as rather inarticulate, modest and religious. He was the son of Ferdinando Lord Fairfax who fought alongside him on a number of occasions. Although his wife had royalist sympathies, Sir Thomas Fairfax had proved a decisive leader in the North where he had raised troops in Yorkshire. Although defeated at Adwalton Moor early in the conflict, he had been with Manchester and Cromwell at the defeat of the royalists at Winceby in Lincolnshire in October 1643, and at Marston Moor he had commanded one group of cavalry and Cromwell the other. Both had been wounded earlier in the battle but their joint decision to pursue the royalists beyond nightfall had secured victory for Parliament. The two houses of Parliament appointed Fairfax General of the New Model Army, but it was not until mid-June, just before Naseby, that

Sir Thomas Fairfax, by an unknown artist (Cromwell Museum, Huntingdon).

Cromwell was appointed his Lieutenant-General. This was on Fairfax's own initiative as Parliament had proved so slow and divided about elevating Cromwell.

Cromwell came from a less aristocratic family than Fairfax. His grandfather, Sir Oliver, had entertained King James at Hinchingbrook House near Huntingdon but frequent visits by the Court had nearly bankrupted him and his son Sir Henry had had to sell the estate to the Montague family, from whom the Earl of Manchester was descended. Cromwell's father, Robert, was the second son and therefore did not inherit the main estate, so falling in status to that of a lesser gentleman. Recent research has suggested that, if Oliver had not inherited lands in Ely in the 1630s, he would have fallen below the rank of gentleman altogether. However, in 1628 he had sat as M.P. for Huntingdon, where he had been born, and then in 1640 for Cambridge. By 1630 he had gone through a religious conversion to a form of Calvinism, coming to believe that his soul was predestined by God for eternal salvation. This made him believe he was one of the elect, those chosen by God to sit on His right hand at the Day of Judgement. He came to believe, like many others, that the Established Church of England was corrupt and needed further reformation, as did the moral lives of the people of England. He was therefore sympathetic to many of the religious groups that emerged in the 1640s who proved more radical than him, but whose members he promoted within the armies of the Eastern Association.

Henry Ireton came from a Nottinghamshire family of gentry and, like Cromwell, had been educated at university (in his case Oxford). He had been a major in Colonel Thornhaugh's horse regiment at Gainsborough and became the Deputy-Governor of the Isle of Ely under Cromwell. Though more intellectual than his superior, having stayed at university longer and having had some legal training at the Middle Temple, he was promoted to being Commissary-General just before Naseby, where he commanded one formation of cavalry. He was returned as a "recruiter M.P.", one of those who was recruited to Parliament in a by-election to fill the place of an absent royalist. Becoming Cromwell's friend and son-in-law, he provided the intellectual clout and ability to draw up petitions and political manifestos that his superior found difficult. Like Cromwell he was Independent in religion, that is he favoured a loosely controlled national church in which independent local congregations of the godly would be virtually self-governing. This structure was opposed by the Presbyterians, who favoured the more tightly-controlled Calvinist system as found in Scotland, but in religious matters the Independents appeared conservative compared with the radical sects.

Henry Ireton, painted by Robert Walker (by courtesy of the National Portrait Gallery, London)

The Grandees were also relatively conservative in politics, all having come from minor aristocratic, gentry or professional backgrounds. They were supported in the army by some middle ranking officers who were Baptists, keen to destroy the old system of Anglican church tithes, which were regarded as property rights by conservatives and some Presbyterians. Other officers, including Colonel Thomas Harrison, were tending towards millenarianism, which preached the imminent thousand-year rule of Christ on earth. To these men the Civil War had been a struggle against the forces of Anti-Christ, the defeat of whom would usher in the Second Coming. Some of these came later to be called the Fifth Monarchy men, as they saw themselves as ushering in the fifth and final monarchy of Christ on earth as foretold in the Book of Revelation. For them, no settlement should include any whom they had defeated, particularly the King. For many in the army its victory over royalism had made it the army of God, whose duty it was to carry out a further reformation both in church and state. Cromwell himself came to believe that God had used the army to carry out his providential plan for the godly, his Chosen People, and that the army should periodically pray for guidance in their political struggles with the various forces ranged against them. In the summer and autumn of 1647, the Grandees found themselves caught between two of these forces, the more conservative Parliament and the more radical Levellers.

The Levellers

Some middle ranking officers, colonels and majors were, like many of their own men, becoming influenced by Leveller doctrines. The Levellers, started out as radical pamphleteers within the City of London. They were labelled 'Levellers' by their critics who were convinced that they were social revolutionaries who wanted to confiscate and redistribute property, thus 'levelling down' society. They disliked the term but, from our point of view, they can be seen as wanting to 'level down' political power, that is to give more people the vote and make political institutions more representative. The most extreme Levellers wanted to abolish the House of Lords and the monarchy and elect a more democratic representative assembly. During 1647 they began to influence the army and gained considerable power when elections to the Army Council took place. Many of the elected agents or agitators were Leveller supporters. The key figures among the 'civilian Levellers' in London were John Lilburne, William Walwyn and Richard Overton. By November 1647 the 'army Levellers' included, Colonels Thomas Rainsborough (Rainborowe) and William Eyre, and Majors Thomas Scott and John Cobbett, all of whom were present at Corkbush Field.

John Lilburne in 1641, from an engraving by George Glover (Bodleian Library, Oxford — Firth.e.63 (2).Frontispiece)

Of these the most celebrated was John Lilburne. He had come as an apprentice to London from County Durham, where his father was a small landowner. He had established a modest brewery but made his name in the 1630s defending the Puritan critics of Charles I and being hauled before the King's courts for importing libellous and seditious books. As a result he was whipped from the Fleet Prison to Westminster and put in the pillory where he had to be gagged to stop him verbally attacking the Bishops. His sufferings and survival in prison led him, like Cromwell, to believe that he was one of God's elect. When the Long Parliament met in 1640 it was Cromwell who spoke up for Lilburne, requesting his release. This was granted so that he could present his case to a parliamentary committee. He later became a Captain in Lord Brook's regiment of foot, which was recruited in London, and he fought at Edgehill and Brentford where he was captured and taken prisoner to Oxford. Though threatened with death, he was reprieved and exchanged for a royalist prisoner, immediately re-enlisting in the Eastern Association army. He became friends with Cromwell who promoted him to be the major in Colonel King's regiment in Lincolnshire. However he quarrelled with King and was transferred to Manchester's regiment. He was promoted Lieutenant-Colonel of Dragoons in 1644 and fought at Marston Moor. He fell out with Manchester and decided to leave the army before Naseby. Thus although he is seen as the leader of the 'civilian Levellers' his military experience was considerable and his reputation as a quarrelsome nuisance already legendary.

John Lilburne had two brothers, Robert and Henry, who also served in the army. Robert Lilburne was the eldest son of Richard Lilburne Esq. of Thickley Puncherdon, County Durham. He had served in both Essex and Manchester's armies as well as raising a regiment of horse in the North. He became a Colonel in the New Model Army and a professional soldier. It was some of the troops from his regiment who mutinied at St. Albans, Luton and Dunstable and came illegally to Corkbush Field and he disassociated himself from his brother John's activities which he must have seen as encouraging the mutiny. Henry, the youngest of the brothers, became a Lieutenant Colonel in Robert's foot regiment and, though later he became Governor of Tynemouth Castle, he defected to the royalists and was killed when the castle was attacked.

In contrast to John Lilburne's confrontational nature, his Leveller colleague, William Walwyn, had avoided self-publicity, issuing radical pamphlets anonymously. He was a Merchant Adventurer from Worcestershire and both a mystic and a sceptical intellectual who worked behind the scenes. The rationalist reformer, Richard Overton, also became identified with Lilburne and Walwyn over 1645 as they printed a series of pamphlets and got into trouble with the Presbyterians in Parliament by attacking the intolerance they saw.   Lilburne was examined by a Commons committee for libelling the Speaker and imprisoned for two months in the autumn, only to be re-arrested by the House of Lords in the following June and put in the Tower.   Overton too was incarcerated for operating an illegal printing press.   However despite the imprisonment of these leaders, the Leveller cause gained influence both in the south-eastern counties and in the army, which was heading for a confrontation with the conservative Presbyterians in Parliament.

The Presbyterian majority in the House of Commons was closely linked to the Scots, who had entered the war on Parliament's side on the understanding that their particular form of Protestant religious government, Calvinist Presbyterianism, would be introduced into England on the ruins of the Anglican church.   However, as the English army contained many who regarded rigid Presbyterianism as much of an enemy to religious toleration as Anglicanism, there was no way that the army would agree to its imposition. The Scots were therefore seeking a deal with the Presbyterians in Parliament and even the King, in order to disband the 'heretic' English army.   It was only the Irish who had united all these opposing groups.   It was the Irish rebellion in 1641 which had accelerated the confrontation in England that led to civil war and they were seen by all other factions as requiring suppression by force.   The army however wished to be able to do this using existing regiments, whereas the Presbyterians in Parliament wanted first to disband the regiments of the New Model Army and then form new ones for the 'Army for Ireland'.   It was this problem that the Levellers exploited.   They knew that by turning the grievance of disbandment (without the payment in full of arrears in the army's pay and expenses) into the principle of 'soldiers' rights' they could gain increasing support among the rank and file.   This was the key issue at the Ware Mutiny and, by gaining support from ordinary soldiers for a radical political programme, they began to divide the army.

The Army Council and the conflict with Parliament

Six key developments took place over the spring and summer of 1647, various strands of which came together at the Ware Mutiny.

— The first was the soldiers' opposition to disbandment and the growth of the Army Council in May, in which elected agents of the soldiers were prominent.

— The second was the apparent plot by the Presbyterians to develop a counter force to the army which led to the seizure of the King by Cornet Joyce in June and Charles being put in the custody of the army.
— The third was the move of the army into the capital following mob riots in London and its threat to impeach the Presbyterian leaders in the Commons.
— The fourth was the development of rival programmes for a political settlement by the officers and the rank and file and discussion of them in the debates at Putney.
— The fifth was the politicisation of the lower ranks of the army by the Levellers and the election of 'new agents' sympathetic to the Levellers in some regiments.
— The sixth was the failure of parliament to find a satisfactory solution to the problem of army pay.

Each development put strains on the relationship between the Grandees and radicals in the lower ranks and helped create an atmosphere in which mutiny could flourish.

The votes for disbanding the army first passed through Parliament in late February. In late March a petition circulated among the officers listing objections to the scheme but this was condemned by Parliament as tending to mutiny. In mid-April, six parliamentary commissioners were sent to the army headquarters, then at Saffron Walden, to persuade the troops to disband and enlist for Ireland. However representatives from eight regiments of cavalry wrote a letter to Fairfax and Cromwell seeking their support for their grievances over pay. Cromwell and Ireton acted as two of four parliamentary commissioners to hear the soldiers grievances and meetings took place in Saffron Walden church between them and representatives of the various regiments. Cromwell reported their views to Parliament in mid-May, informing M.P.s that the soldiers would probably disband if ordered, but would not enlist for Ireland. Despite offering only eight weeks back pay, Parliament went ahead to fix the dates for the disbanding of the regiments. In order to present their grievances, representatives were chosen from the cavalry and foot regiments as well, and this meeting turned into an Army Council — or the General Council of the Army, as it called itself. The Army Council included the senior officers and elected agents or agitators, as they were called, from each regiment. These men kept in touch, not just with other regiments in the North but also with supporters in London, organising the soldiers to resist disbandment and using portable printing presses to issue pamphlets putting their case to a wider audience.

A woodcut of Sir Thomas Fairfax and the Council of the Army in 1647 (By permission of The British Library — Thomason Tracts, E409/25)

When the Army Council met at Bury St. Edmunds at the end of May, the agitators of 16 regiments petitioned Fairfax to fix a rendezvous for the whole of the army. His own regiment was supposed to be disbanded on the 1st June but, as the Grandees were sympathetic to the soldiers' grievances, the latter ignored the orders to disband and marched to the rendezvous on Kentford Heath, east of Newmarket. The artillery, which was ordered to go to Parliament in London was seized at Oxford for the army, and soldiers under Cornet Joyce went on to seize the King from the parliamentary commissioners at Holdenby House. This appears to have been known to the Grandees, but subsequently Joyce, on his own initiative took the King to join the army at Newmarket. All of these actions would in other circumstances have been deemed mutinous, and were so by some in Parliament. Cromwell's critics saw them as part of an ambitious scheme inspired by him, but it seems that like others he was reacting to the initiative of lower ranking officers and to the uncovering of a plot by eleven Presbyterian leaders in Parliament to do a deal with the Scots to bring in their army and re-establish the King on the Presbyterian and Scots' terms.

By early June, therefore, the army was united in its opposition to the threat from Parliament and those officers who had sided with Parliament or had agreed to go to Ireland were replaced by men directly loyal to the Grandees. General Poyntz, the commander of the Northern Association army — a separate organisation from the New Model Army — was arrested by his own men and his forces subsequently integrated into Fairfax's. The Grandees called together all the available regiments on Kentford Heath, east of Newmarket, on the 4th and 5th June and, as a result, drew up a document known as *A Solemn Engagement of the Army*. A week later on the 10th June at Thriplow Heath, east of Royston, the soldiers supported this document and agreed not to disband or be divided until their just demands had been met. Cromwell, however, was an M.P. as well as a Grandee, and on the 16th May he had still been urging his fellow officers to accept a parliamentary settlement. Although the politicisation of the army in the previous few months had made this very difficult, Cromwell still hoped for a compromise over the next five months, keeping in touch with the more radical Independents in the Parliament who supported the claims of the army. His subordinate Henry Ireton helped draw up a further manifesto from the officers on 14th June called *The Representation of the Army*. This attempted to produce a balanced programme of reform, including calls for the impeachment of the eleven Presbyterian leaders, liberty for tender consciences — but not religious licence — regular elections for Parliament but also a place for the King in a final settlement.

Above: St. Mary's Church, Putney, where the debates were held (Guildhall Library, Corporation of London)
Below: Colonel Thomas Rainsborough (Cromwell Museum, Huntingdon)

During the latter part of June, the army crossed Hertfordshire (see below) and by July was quartered at Reading where it developed its own ideas for a political settlement, *The Heads of the Proposals*. The exact authorship of this is now in dispute, many historians believing it to be largely Ireton's work, others that of an aristocratic supporter, Lord Saye and Sele. At Reading the agitators wanted to march on London and impose their own settlement on Parliament, but Cromwell attempted to stop them. However events took over and a mob in London, with the apparent collusion of the Presbyterian leaders, invaded the House of Commons and forced the M.P.s to request that the King go to London. As a result the army occupied the capital on the 6th August. The Grandees still kept in touch with the King, hoping that he would accept the *Heads of the Proposals* as a basis for a settlement while their political allies in the Lords introduced sections of them as bills in Parliament. Over the summer and early autumn, the King was moved by the army to a number of houses and eventually to Hampton Court, but never into London where it was feared popular royalism would flourish. The Levellers, despite Lilburne's continued imprisonment, had also been active and produced a rival document to the *Heads of the Proposals* which they presented at the Army Council when it met at Putney.

An Agreement of the People and the Putney Debates

At the meetings of the Army Council in Putney church in October and early November, Cromwell and Ireton were presented with a paper called *An Agreement of the People*. This was a draft set of principles for a new constitution for England and the Levellers' answer to the Grandees' proposals. It was clear from these 'Putney Debates' that the Generals did not agree with many of the principles in the *Agreement*. Cromwell presided in Fairfax's absence through illness and he and Ireton put the case for the Grandees. Those presenting or speaking on behalf of the *Agreement* included Colonel Rainsborough, Edward Sexby, John Wildman and a number of middle-rank officers.

Rainsborough was the son of a naval captain and had himself served in the navy at the start of the war. He then became a Colonel, raising a regiment for Manchester's army, and had been briefly captured while defending Hull. He recaptured Crowland Abbey near Peterborough and was subsequently put in command of an infantry regiment in the New Model Army. He distinguished himself in a series of battles and sieges at Naseby, Bristol, Oxford and Worcester. He became a recruiter M.P. in 1646 and was in Parliament, absent

John Wildman (Cromwell Museum, Huntingdon)

from his regiment, in 1647 when it mutinied and refused to be sent to Jersey. He then joined the army radicals and Levellers in their protests and occupied Southwark when the army marched on London in August.   In the Putney Debates, where on the second day he and Ireton dominated the proceedings, Rainsborough took up a near democratic position, arguing that even the poorest man should have a vote.

John Wildman has been ranked both with the civilian Levellers and the army radicals and was probably a link between the two.   He is said to have been at Cambridge, had some legal training and was probably brought in by the Levellers to help them draft their petitions and manifestos.   He and Edward Sexby were probably responsible for refining the documents presented at Putney.   Sexby has been seen as the leader of the agitators, having been in Cromwell's then Fairfax's regiments.   He was in constant touch with Lilburne providing him with writing materials and getting his pamphlets printed.   Some historians have assumed that Lilburne, who was still imprisoned in the Tower of London on the orders of the House of Lords, also had a hand in writing the *Agreement*. The paper was a summary of a much longer pamphlet *The Case of the Army Truly Stated*, which had been drawn up by some newly-elected agents from five horse regiments. The *Agreement* had been printed by the 3rd November and it was folded into the hat bands of some of the soldiers in the regiments which turned up, against orders, at Corkbush Field. John Lilburne, who had been allowed out of the Tower for the day, possibly on the excuse of seeing his lawyer, is reported as being at an inn in Ware on the 15th November, the day of the mutiny.

The *Agreement* therefore had a particular significance for the Ware Mutiny. It was both the cause of the break-up of the Army Council on 9th November, that led to the decision to call three separate rendezvous of the army, the first being at Ware, and it was the reason why Fairfax suppressed the mutineers. Why was it that the Grandees found it so unacceptable? The writers of the *Agreement*, as can be seen in the accounts of the debates at Putney, assumed that the old regime had ended, that the old unwritten constitution and system of law and government was finished and that the 'free-born people of England' were entitled to decide what the new political set-up should be. For the Levellers, 'free-born people' included all those who had lost their freedom in previous generations, but had regained it by fighting for it in the civil war. Some even argued that all laws and distribution of property since the Norman Conquest should be declared invalid. The Grandees could not accept any of this. They were gentlemen of property, steeped in the traditional view of property rights protected by the existing law. What the *Agreement* suggested to them was that, if implemented, it would allow the election of those with no property by those with no property, who would then pass laws to redistribute property. The Generals held power from Parliament, and were not yet prepared to overthrow it by a revolutionary act declaring that the present parliamentary regime had to come to an end. The Putney Debates and the Ware Mutiny thus witnessed a clash of ideologies. On the one side were the Grandees, whose social and legal ideas were relatively conservative, and on the other the Levellers and their supporters, whose radical political ideas led them to believe they could establish a new legal and constitutional system. After the inconclusive debates at Putney, the Grandees decided not to assemble the whole army in one place but to hold the first of three rendezvous for one brigade at Corkbush Field to regain full control of the regiments. To the agitators and their Leveller supporters, this would divide the army and go against the *Solemn Engagement of the Army*, to which the whole army had pledged itself at Kentford and Thriplow Heaths in June. However they saw greater danger in the attitude of Parliament.

The soldiers and Parliament

Apart from a desire to obtain their arrears of pay and a commitment to "England's Freedoms and Soldiers' Rights" — the slogan printed on the back of the latest edition of the *Agreement,* why was it that soldiers from Colonel Harrison's and Colonel Lilburne's regiments decided to disobey orders by coming to the Ware rendezvous and risk the consequences?   Part of the explanation may be in the nature of the administration of parliamentary finances and the apparent failure of Parliament to agree a pay formula.   It would seem that soldiers were determined to get to the first rendezvous, in case the other two never took place and they thus lost any chance of getting back pay.   London was seen as the source of money, since that is where their paymasters, the parliamentary treasurers, lived and organised their finances. Orders to march north took them away from the only likely source of income. Previous armies had been regional, like that of the Eastern Association, and had been paid locally from Cambridge. The New Model Army was a national army paid from London. Though this originally had advantages, by late 1647 its main disadvantage was that no soldier, whose pay was months in arrears, was willing to leave the Home Counties.

The Generals had clearly sensed at Putney that the regiments would remain restless until pay was forthcoming. They continually put pressure on Parliament, which seemed to be spending more time and energy on working out new propositions to put to the King than on soldiers' pay.   The return of the officer M.P.s from the Army Council to Parliament began to have an effect. On the 18th October both Ireton and Thomas Scott were added to a parliamentary committee to discuss the ninth proposition to put to the King and on the 22nd October a committee was established to discuss how the arrears of the army might be secured.   The membership of this committee included both Cromwell and Rainsborough as well as four M.P.s from Hertfordshire: Sir William Lytton of Knebworth, Sir Thomas Dacres of Cheshunt, William Priestly of Essendon and Captain Edward Wingate from Welwyn. Thus two of the Generals and two of the Leveller sympathisers were intimately involved with finding solutions to the main political and financial issues. However it is significant that M.P.s from the communities which had suffered most from 'free quarter' were strongly represented on the Committee for arrears and this seems to have had an important effect.

The next day, the 23rd October, it was agreed that £150,000 was to be paid to the Treasurers at War for payment to the army out of the excise duties or, if this was insufficient, they were to raise loans on the credit of the excise. Two days later it was agreed that soldiers were to be paid out of the income from the lands confiscated from the bishops. On the 2nd November the House of Commons turned itself into a Grand Committee under Colonel White to take into consideration the whole question of raising money for the army. Thus by the beginning of the month the soldiers' expectations were being raised and it looked as if Parliament was finally going to do something about their pay. The Generals by this time were concerned about the potentially mutinous state of the army and a decision was made by Wednesday 10th November that the army would be called together on the first three days of the following week. This plan was probably designed to prevent mass opposition, following the unsatisfactory conclusion to the Putney debates, and to disperse the soldiers so that no one area suffered continually from free quarter. However the plan appears to have backfired.

The rendezvous at Corkbush Field came at a time when all the factions jockeying for power in the post-war period were divided. Parliament was split and some of the more conservative peers were being threatened with a treason trial because of their actions earlier in the summer. The army was divided between conservatives and radicals in both religion and politics. It encompassed various religious sects and groupings: Independents, Presbyterians, Baptists, and those who looked forward to the imminent Second Coming of Christ on earth and establishment of the rule of 'the godly saints'. It was also divided between those who wanted to get rid of the entire constitution as it had developed since the Middle Ages and to return to a mythical state of pre-Norman freedom, those who wanted merely to limit the monarch's powers by continuing negotiations with the King, and those who saw him as the 'man of blood' who should be put on trial. However they were united in believing that God was on their side, as he had so far blessed their endeavours in their struggle against the King. In addition to providing an opportunity for the Generals to unite the disparate groups within the army, Corkbush Field was also important because it gave the Generals an opportunity to make an example of soldiers who had mutinied against their officers a few days before at St. Albans, Luton and Dunstable and, contrary to orders, come to the rendezvous.

The 'Moving Mutiny' — St. Albans, Luton and Dunstable

The events at St. Albans, Luton and Dunstable began on the 23rd October, the day when Parliament agreed to raise £150,000 for soldiers' pay from the

S.Cooper pinxt.   C.Watson sculp

ROBERT   **LILBURNE,**

Heir of the ancient Family *of Lilburne of Thickley*

Puncherdon, in the *Bishoprick of Durham;*

IN THE GRAND REBELLION;

Colonel of Horse, Major General of the North of England

Commander in Chief in Scotland

and one of the Regicides

Born 1613.

Died, a Prisoner in St. Nicholas Island, Plymouth,

August 1665.

From an Original Picture in the Possession of Mr R. Graves:

N.B. He was Elder Brother of the Fanatic John Lilburne.

London, Published 1st May 1807, by Rt. Wilkinson No. 58 Cornhill.

Robert Lilburne, from a miniature by Samuel Cooper with text added in the early nineteenth century (by courtesy of the Curators of the Ashmolean Museum, Oxford) excise. Part of what happened over the subsequent three weeks can be pieced together from accounts at the time and later statements by Captain-Lieutenant William Bray, of Robert Lilburne's regiment, the most senior officer to march with his troops to Corkbush Field, contrary to orders, and those of Henry Lilburne and other officers of the regiment. Though Robert Lilburne, recently appointed Governor of Newcastle, was a Baptist and opposed to the rigid Presbyterianism of the conservatives in Parliament, he was no Leveller and disassociated himself from the activities of his brother John and those of his own men. Robert Lilburne ordered the regiment to go northwards, to Newcastle, but the soldiers were reluctant to do so as they hoped to be paid. When they reached St. Albans, the Leveller pamphlet, *The Case of the Army Truly Stated* was read to them, presumably by one of the London Agents. Henry Lilburne later stated that the mutiny first started at St. Albans among the Colonel's own company. Other companies in the regiment had already moved up the Dunstable road and became strung out along the Bedfordshire/Buckinghamshire border. According to Bray, a Council of War was held at the village of Hockcliffe, a few miles north-west of Dunstable, after which he tried to persuade his company to continue marching northwards. They reached Olney but refused to go any farther, and on being joined by other troops from Northamptonshire, including some discontented cavalry, they began to march back to Dunstable. There two contrary influences were brought to bear upon them, the action of their officers and the influence of the Levellers.

Henry Lilburne and his Major, Hobson, who by the 28th October had gone to Fairfax for advice, returned with fresh orders for the men to march north and also brought some money which was to be distributed among the regiment. The officers decided that the captains, including Bray, should persuade the men to march back into Buckinghamshire and some money was accordingly given to the captains. After a number of meetings and what were described as "various outrages against their officers and the countryfolk", the captains found that soldiers in Captain Tolhurst's company at Luton had seized him and his money. In the skirmish to force his release, two men were killed and a lieutenant had his hand slashed off. Henry Lilburne later claimed that some of the officers were:

> pursued many miles by their owne Souldiers, who swore as they pursued them, they would be revenged on them, and did violently take away divers horses in the countrey in this pursuit of their Officers, pretending their Officers were run away with their money, when they were forced to run to save their lives, there being one Lieutenant dangerously wounded by them.

Henry Lilburne's version is supported by evidence from the St. Albans Mayor's Accounts, which refer to expenses for "fetchinge backe from Luton fower horses which the souldiers hadde away thither". Though Bray's and Henry Lilburne's accounts differ in relation to the part that Bray played, they seem agreed that Leveller and possibly royalist influences were also at work.

London Agents had arrived in Dunstable with the letter headed *England's Freedoms, Soldiers' Rights*, which presumably included within it a copy of *An Agreement of the People*. The distributors of this letter led the soldiers to believe that if they marched further south, then Fairfax and Cromwell would not oppose them and that they would be dividing the army by moved northwards. Royalist infiltrators also seem to have been at work, claiming that they should march south since the King would join them at the rendezvous. The report in the Clarke Papers of the 3rd November (the official record of the meetings of the Army Council and senior officers) is terse and to the point:

> 400 of Col. Lilburne's Regiment declared for the Kinge, upon their coming back to Dunstable, offering the countrymen their arms, and they would take clubs, and bringe the Kinge to Whitehall. They would see what their officers would doe, and then they would carry the Kinge away.

A report two days later said the regiment had thrown off all their officers and another on the 9th November indicated that Fairfax intended to "chastize the regiment that hath discharged themselves of their officers".

Sir Lewis Dyve, a royalist prisoner in the Tower of London, wrote to King Charles on Thursday the 28th October and referred to the mutiny as starting on the previous Saturday, i.e. 23rd October. The fact that royalists were so well informed suggests that they did have an influence on this moving mutiny. This date was also the day after *The Case of the Army Truly Stated* had been discussed for the first time in the Army Council. It was well before the fixing of the date for the Ware Rendezvous, so that the cause of the initial mutiny must have been the fact that the soldiers were being sent to the North — though they were later influenced by royalists and Levellers. To the militants in the army, the decision to send them north was seen as dividing the army and going against the principles of the June *Engagement* at Newmarket. Hearing later that there was to be a rendezvous at Ware, they probably suspected that some more money would be available to the regiments that attended, and so resolved to disobey orders and march south again.

Given that some of the soldiers of the New Model Army had previously fought for the King, but had deserted to Parliament for better pay, the combination of calls for army solidarity and populist royalism was a heady mixture. Other royalists in London had heard of problems among the soldiers at Dunstable as early as the 4th November and also reports of disturbances over pay at St. Albans and Luton. Their agents might well have tried to foment dissent in order to weaken the army. The day before the Corkbush Field rendezvous, most of Robert Lilburne's Regiment minus many of its officers had marched south from Dunstable to Redbourn and St. Albans, determined to get to Ware at some time on the next day. Henry Lilburne admitted later that, if it had not been for Captain Bray and his Quartermaster holding the men back, they would have plundered the town.

Bray however had gone back to Putney the previous week, as he spoke in the discussions on the 8th November. Cromwell had said that the first clause of the *Agreement* "did tend very much to Anarchy", and Bray "made a long speech to take off what the Lieut. General said, that what hee call'd Anarchy, was for propriety" (i.e. property). It was after this exchange, that it was decided to call the rendezvous, though Bray may well have left by then since he did not sign the resolution. Bray admitted that when he returned to his own company all the colours of the regiment had been gathered together at St. Albans. Though the self-justificatory comments in his subsequent narrative of events cannot be taken as hard evidence for his actions, there is enough supporting evidence to suggest that his outline of events is probably close to the truth. Whether he went to the rendezvous as commander of a mutiny or, as he put it, "to hinder an unjust influence" is still open to question. There is also a report in a news-sheet that, just hours before the rendezvous was due to take place, Colonel Rainsborough warned Parliament that, unless money was provided for the soldiers present, trouble might ensue. Postponement of the rendezvous was debated, but it was clearly too late as the soldiers were already assembling. Thus, expectations about pay had been raised among the soldiers and because of poor, contradictory or inaccurate communication, one of two key regiments decided, against orders, to march to Ware. The reason why the other key regiment, that of Col. Harrison, decided to attend against orders are not recorded in any detail and are more obscure.

The plans for the Rendezvous

One reason for the uncertainty as to which regiments could legitimately turn up at Ware may lie in this question of inadequate communication. The

Generals were secretive about the venues of the subsequent rendezvous, the various news-sheet editors were willing to spread any rumour they heard and the soldiers were consequently anxious and confused. It was reported in one of the parliamentary news-sheets that, although the first rendezvous would be at Ware, it was not fully resolved where the others would be. A rumour the next day said that the general rendezvous would be at Ware on Monday followed by others at Kingston, Watford and Rickmansworth. On the 11th a news-sheet put out the rumour that the second rendezvous would be at St. Albans and the third at Kingston. On the 12th November Fairfax wrote to Parliament from Putney saying he was going the next day to Ware and would stay there till Monday. The next day a news-sheet thought as many as 15 regiments might be going to Ware. In fact the second rendezvous took place at Ruislip Heath on the 17th and the third at Hain or Hare Warren near Kingston upon Thames. The confusion that must have resulted from these various rumours explains why many soldiers would have been keen to get to the first rendezvous.

3
The Immediate Context

General Sir Thomas Fairfax and Hertfordshire

The Ware Mutiny has been viewed by some historians as part of the history of the Levellers, when their supporters in the army were suppressed by the Generals.   Others have seen it as an incident in the career of Oliver Cromwell, when he put down opposition within the ranks that threatened his rise to power.   However two features of it are important in understanding the overall historical context.   First, there is evidence that some of the soldiers court-martialled afterwards may have been sentenced, not for what they did on the day at Ware, but for what had occurred previously at St. Albans, Luton and Dunstable.   Secondly it was General Fairfax, as commander-in-chief, who was the ultimate authority on the day and the events have to be seen in relation to his negotiations with Parliament over all the grievances of the army as well as the Grandees' relationship with the junior officers, ordinary soldiers and 'levelling agents'.   At the time, Cromwell was only second-in-command and his role may have been exaggerated because of his later rise to power as Lord Protector in the 1650s.

Part of the historical context of the Ware Mutiny which needs to be grasped is the army's relationships with the local authorities in the Home Counties and the City of London.   Both the capital and counties like Hertfordshire had supported Parliament throughout the conflict, but many had been complaining for years about the burden of taxation required to pay for the army and the burden of free quarter taken by the army.   Free quarter involved the soldiers living in the homes of ordinary people without payment for board and lodging and then giving the householders an I.O.U., which could in theory, be cashed in at a later stage. The army was dependent on retaining the goodwill of those communities in the Home Counties which fed and housed them. General Fairfax had been very careful to build up good relationships with the local authorities, particularly in Hertfordshire, where soldiers had taken free quarter in winter ever since the start of the war.   Before reaching Putney, the army had spent much of the summer and early autumn in Essex and Hertfordshire and would have been well aware of a range of local grievances, against both the Parliament and army.   Fairfax had been at Royston on the 11th June when he requested a month's pay to be sent in advance to St. Albans, as he did not want to levy any money on the local people. This, he said, would be unacceptable to him and the whole army. The army in return made it clear it would try and avoid interrupting trade to London and increasing the local price of food.

Parliament, afraid of the power and influence of the army, had persuaded it to keep out of the capital, while at the same time promising to raise money to pay off its arrears. Conservative Presbyterians in London tried to raise their own forces to defend the capital and to counteract the army but when they sought the support of the Hertfordshire Militia, Gabriel Barbour, the

DANIEL AXTEL,
Executed at Tyburn,1660.

Daniel Axtell (Cromwell Museum, Huntingdon)

Chairman of the Hertford Militia Committee, sided with Fairfax and rendezvoused the local militia at Watford. Having been assured of their support, Fairfax moved into the capital in August to restore the Independent M.P.s, who had fled from Parliament to the army while the London mob had controlled the streets. Although the army withdrew, the patience of many, including the Generals, was running out. On the 8th November, a week before the Mutiny at Ware, the General Council of the Army sent proposals to Parliament for a financial settlement. They included requests for up to six weeks pay, guarantees for arrears to be backed up by income from estates belonging to the Church and delinquent royalists and, thirdly, provision for permanent pay "to avoid the oppression of the people by free quarter, than which, nothing is more grievous to us". So important was free quarter as an issue that Fairfax was prepared to contemplate imposing the death sentence on any soldier who took it by force.

The day after these proposals were sent, a number of soldiers in Colonel

Hewson's regiment — including his Lieutenant-Colonel, the Baptist Daniel Axtell from Berkhamsted — sent a remonstrance to Fairfax saying they saw him as a "choice instrument" of God's glory and would support him in opposing and suppressing all incendiaries "who do and shall begat dismay and distemper in the army". Thus a week before the rendezvous at Ware, Fairfax felt he had responded to local concerns over the issue of free quarter, and was assured of local support in Hertfordshire, as well as from key regiments like Hewson's. It is significant that it was Hewson's regiment, in which Fairfax had confidence, that he planned to send into London after the Mutiny to obtain the arrears in taxation.

Why it was decided to call the first rendezvous near Ware has never been fully explained. However there are a number of possible explanations. First, Ware was on the Old North Road and therefore had direct access to the City of London. This would be an advantage if, because of a change in circumstances, it was decided to move rapidly on the capital. Secondly both Ware and Hertford had many inns and taverns and were therefore able to accommodate the officers. Thirdly the area was well known to the army as troops had quartered there in the winters of 1643-4 and in the early summer of 1645 when Hertfordshire had been used as an assembly point for the newly formed regiments before the Battle of Naseby, and Fairfax's own regiment had recently been stationed around Ware. Fourthly the local authorities in Hertfordshire had recently shown their loyalty to Fairfax when, on the 5th August, they had sent a delegation to him offering him the support of two regiments of trained bands, each consisting of 1300 men and two troops of horse. Gabriel Barbour, the chairman of the local militia committee was a former mayor of Hertford, a merchant and London property developer, who had largely been responsible for managing the county's war effort. Two regiments of local volunteers had been raised in the early months of hostilities and, though some of these were no longer professional soldiers, the trained bands probably contained enough experienced men for this to be more than a scratch force. On the 29th October Fairfax had also received a petition from Hertfordshire pressing for "settlement of the kingdom according to the declarations of the army". This implies that Fairfax had carefully nurtured support for the army's views on how the constitutional settlement should be organised. Fifthly, the local inhabitants in Hertford and Ware were under the influence of Independent preachers and magistrates like Barbour. Their religious position was thus similar to that of the army generals. More extreme forms of Baptist preaching had grown up in West Hertfordshire and East Buckinghamshire, and a petition to Parliament the year before from the

Above: The Salisbury Arms (formerly The Bell), Hertford, where Fairfax and the senior officers probably stayed before the rendezvous.
Below: An engraving of Ware High Street in the early nineteenth century — it would have changed little since the seventeenth century. (Ware Museum)

Chiltern area suggested it was also more radical politically. It was thus safer to have the first rendezvous away from Putney, and in East rather than West Hertfordshire.

The senior officers were housed in Hertford, probably at the Bell Inn, which had been the place where parliamentary committees had met and where magistrates had convened their monthly meetings before the war. Although it was the county town and had a thriving corn market, it was not economically as important as Ware, three miles to the east, which was a major transhipment point for grain and malt. Grain from Cambridgeshire and malt from all parts of North and East Hertfordshire came down the Old North Road and large quantities were transferred to barge and taken down the River Lea to London. Supplies for large numbers of troops would therefore be easily available. Conveniently situated one day's coach journey out of London on the road to York, the town had a large number of inns, taverns and alehouses. It could therefore house and feed many of the soldiers already quartered or assembling in the surrounding areas. The contrast between the two towns also reflected the hierarchy within the army. Hertford was an incorporated borough with a Mayor, Corporation and its own parliamentary representation. It had been under the influence of William the second Earl of Salisbury, one of the aristocratic allies of the Independents in the army. Its town government thus represented a more formalised notion of hierarchy and order, whereas Ware was unincorporated, relied on parochial officials for its administration, sprawled over the river into the neighbouring parish of Great Amwell and had been in conflict in the 1630s with the local royalist landowners, the Fanshawes of Ware Park. It had also been in conflict with its rival Hertford particularly over access on the river between the two towns. It is not surprising therefore that on the day of the rendezvous John Lilburne found an inn in Ware more congenial than going to Hertford.

However taking the army back into Hertfordshire looked like a gamble, as some of the local troops raised in early August in support of Fairfax had themselves mutinied. The treasurer of the Hertford Militia Committee, William Turner, later submitted his expenditure for 1647 to the parliamentary sub-committee of accounts for scrutiny. In August and September he recorded expenses for the payment of these troops noting however "at which time beinge in harvest the footemen had 12d. per diem, which by reason of their mutinie the committee could not avoid the payment of". The Hertfordshire volunteer regiments had earlier in the war deserted their garrisons to bring in the harvest, and presumably would only serve the county again if they were paid a rate equivalent to or higher than the labourer's wage at harvest time. Fairfax however may have felt confident in the local committee because of their handling of this earlier mutiny. A Marshall had been called from the main army, the mutineers had been arrested by John Pennyfather and Thomas Herrick and sent up to London under guard. Major Barbour, the son of Gabriel Barbour, and a senior officer in the local cavalry, had spent a month prosecuting the mutineers at army headquarters. Fairfax therefore knew that, having already purged the local troops of troublemakers, Hertfordshire would be a relatively safe place to hold a rendezvous.

Fairfax had also come to rely on the support of the Hertfordshire authorities as a result of the activities of Major Francis White of the General's own foot regiment. White had been removed from the Army Council in September because of inflammatory remarks he had made as the elected agitator for the regiment on a joint committee between the Army Council and a group of M.P.s. By mid-October, the regiment had moved from Surrey to Hertfordshire where White wrote a letter to the other officers of the regiment, who by the 16th October were stationed at Ware. Although he tried to justify his actions, the letter revealed his sympathy for the Levellers. He wrote:

> there is no forme of government by Divine Appointment, but the voice
> of the people is the voice of God, as much for one as another, and that
> is the most legall and just authoritie which is set up by consent.

These views reached the soldiers, who seemed more affected by populist royalism than by Leveller ideas and a minor mutiny appears to have taken place at Ware eleven days before the main one. In William Turner's treasurer's accounts for Hertfordshire, there is an order dated the 6th November and signed by Gabriel Barbour for him to pay seven shillings to the:

> guard of soldiers that came to Hertford by the appointment of a councell
> of warre to see some offenders of Major White's company in the
> General's regiment, punished.

This probably relates to an incident that took place on Thursday the 4th November, as reported in a newsletter in the Clarendon Papers:

> On Thursday last Sir Thomas Fairfax's regiment of foot were drawn to
> a rendezvous; and one White, the Major of the regiment, told the soldiers
> that the kingdom must be under another government (which he said to
> see how they would like it). Whereupon the whole regiment threw up
> their hats and cried, 'A King, A King'. And thereupon White got to his
> horse and made some haste out of the field.

King Charles I in three positions, painted by Van Dyck. (The Royal Collection © Her Majesty The Queen)

Fairfax was clearly having ongoing problems with awkward officers, nascent mutiny and popular royalism within his own regiment and felt by reviewing his troops near Hertford he would be able to rely on the local authorities who were prepared to back him. Popular royalism was always a problem but especially after the escape of the King from Hampton Court on the 11th November.

The escape of King Charles

The rendezvous at Corkbush Field can be seen as partly an attempt by the Generals to restore unity within the army at a place of their own choosing and partly a stage in their campaign to put pressure on Parliament. It was also

Charles I held prisoner in Carisbrooke Castle on the Isle of Wight, where he fled in November 1647 — from a Royalist broadsheet of the time. (Bodleian Library, Oxford — C.15.3.Linc.(2).Title page.)

essential that the various divisions in the army were kept in check because of a new threat posed by the King. Charles had been defeated, but had been kept under guard at Hampton Court since August while negotiations with Parliament continued. For reasons which are still obscure, the King was able to escape to the Isle of Wight, where he was then held at Carisbrooke Castle by the new Governor, Robin Hammond, a distant relative of Cromwell's. Contemporaries and historians, critical of Cromwell's motives, have assumed that he had allowed the King to escape, knowing that his relative, who had been recently appointed to the post, would secure him. This they argued strengthened his hand as it meant he had a secure hold over the King away from the influence of the Scots, the Levellers and Parliament. However the risks involved in such an enterprise were not those that Cromwell usually took. The notion that, by raising the spectre of a King on the loose Cromwell would immediately be able to unite the army, was a gamble that was out of character.

The Generals were concerned about the Levellers and rumours were flying around of a plot by the more extreme elements in the army to murder the King.

An anonymous letter dated the 9th November was found on a table in the King's room the next morning, which gave news of a meeting of the agitators on the 8th at which they and the two army chaplains, Peter and Dell, were alleged to have plotted to murder the King. Though this may well have been a piece of planted evidence — and Peter and Dell vehemently protested at a similar falsehood in a letter published a few days later — there was always a possibility that the Levellers might have tried to capture the King to use him as a bargaining card against the Grandees, as events at Dunstable described above suggest. Cromwell and Colonel Edward Whalley, who was in charge of the guard, had removed some of the King's advisers a few days before, fearing a royalist escape plot, but had allowed the King whom they still held in respect relative freedom within Hampton Court. Rainsborough suspected a plot by Cromwell and even suggested, before the news of the King's arrival on the Isle of Wight, that he might still be hidden at Hampton Court.

However, the Generals were not expecting Charles to escape and it was important for them to hold on to the King, since this gave them greater bargaining power in their negotiations with Parliament. The Scots had a keener interest in seeing the King freed from the Generals' immediate control, as can be seen by their secret negotiations later. Charles' escape to the Isle of Wight was poorly planned and very much a last minute affair. He had originally hoped to get to the Channel Islands or France but eventually decided on the Isle of Wight as no other route was available, and he believed that Robin Hammond the Governor would be sympathetic to him as he was the brother of a royal chaplain. That Cromwell was not expecting him to go to the Isle of Wight is seen from the fact that the army had later to send extra troops there, as the local gentry were proving rather too sympathetic to the King. Popular royalism was on the increase and the Levellers were trying to use it as a weapon in their struggle against both the Parliament and Grandees.

Leveller intentions

The reasons why the Levellers and their supporters decided to make a show of defiance at Ware are probably related to their belief that they had considerable support in the area and in the army and also because they needed to counter the opposition to *An Agreement of the People* recently voiced in the Army Council and in the House of Commons, which had condemned it. In

August a pamphlet from radicals in the county attacked the "self-seeking Parliament" and the "company of treacherous Aldermen" in the City of London. On the 14th September a petition was published by Leveller supporters in Hertfordshire, Buckinghamshire and Oxfordshire, in which they called for Lilburne to be released from the Tower and for constant pay for the army to be provided in an equal way. Christopher Feake, who had been vicar of All Saints' Church in Hertford, was well known as a supporter of Lilburne. There had been considerable agitation against tithes in the county for over a year and the Leveller leaders may have thought that they could capitalise on that. They believed that they had support in the army because of the apparent success of the new agents in influencing the lower ranks. They believed that by playing on the soldiers' anxieties over pay and the local people's dislike of free quarter, they might unite them. Although they had largely won the argument at Putney, they had no public forum outside the Army Council. When they arrived at Corkbush Field they not only had a newly-printed edition of *An Agreement of the People* already distributed, but they also had a *Humble Petition* from officers and soldiers to present to Fairfax.

In this petition they expressed their views in forthright terms which Fairfax and Cromwell could not ignore. They claimed that the soldiers had fought with Fairfax against the royalists "to preserve and vindicate the freedoms of our native country and of the Parliament" and to secure "to us and all the freeborn people their native rights". The only way they could see of doing this was to get all to subscribe to the *Agreement* and for the army to remain united in one body. They sought Fairfax's support for the *Agreement* and asked that he continue as their commander-in-chief. This attempt to get round the other senior officers, such as Ireton and Cromwell, and to appeal directly to the overall commander was either naive or a cynical attempt to use the traditional form of petition to state their case yet again. They knew that it was bound to be rejected, yet would nevertheless gain publicity as it would be reported to and probably discussed in Parliament. The reaction of the House of Lords to the petition and *Agreement* was to be expected. They were referred to the committee investigating the whole mutiny and it was ordered that a declaration should be prepared showing the House's dislike of them. The Commons had already seen a copy of the *Agreement* on the 9th November and had condemned it as "destructive to the being of Parliaments and to the fundamental government of the kingdom". Both houses clearly believed that John Lilburne was the key figure behind the scenes in the production of these pamphlets.

The role of John Lilburne and the 'New Agents'

John Lilburne, the established leader of the London Levellers had been imprisoned in the Tower of London since July 1646 for a pamphlet attacking the House of Lords, but had encouraged the Leveller supporters in the army throughout the summer and autumn of 1647. He had been disappointed at not being released by the army when it had moved into London in August and had turned against Cromwell, whom he had expected would secure his release. It was Lilburne who had been behind the election of the new agents, suspecting that the old agitators had been bought off by Cromwell. He was also, because of lax security in the Tower, able to talk to royalist prisoners and he may have encouraged the dangerous mixture of Leveller agitation and popular royalism to get back at the Grandees. Somehow he also managed to persuade Parliament on the 9th November that he should "have his Liberty every day to go without his keeper to attend the Committee about his business and return every night to the Tower". This Committee had been considering his case for over twelve months. Given Lilburne's reputation and previous activities, this system of day-release was rather rash, because it enabled him to organise supporters in the City in advance of the rendezvous.

The Levellers in the City called a number of meetings at two taverns in the East End, the *Mouth* at Aldersgate and the *Windmill* in Coleman Street along the Mile End Road. They appear to have been trying to whip up support among the populace to attend the rendezvous at Ware. On the 10th November Tobias Box, one of the agitators of Colonel Horton's regiment, was reported as being at a meeting at the *Mouth* the night before and then arrested and taken before the Lord Mayor for being on the streets at an unreasonable hour of the night. The atmosphere of alarm was probably heightened by a continuance of an attack of the plague, which had killed 120 in the City alone in the previous week. On the 13th November, 150 weavers were reported as attending a meeting at the *Mouth* with the intention of marching to Ware two days later. One report suggested that the plan was to attend the rendezvous in order to present Fairfax with a petition for the redress of grievances. The new agents had also distributed pamphlets in the City demanding a General Rendezvous of the army, i.e. for one to be attended by all regiments, not just the seven called to Corkbush Field. Twistleton's regiment at Cambridge and Ireton's to the west appear to have been in favour of this. A copy of this pamphlet, signed by Edward Sexby, the radical spokesman at Putney, by Joseph Aleyn of Harrison's regiment and by no less than five representatives of Robert Lilburne's regiment, reveals the hardened attitude of the new agents towards

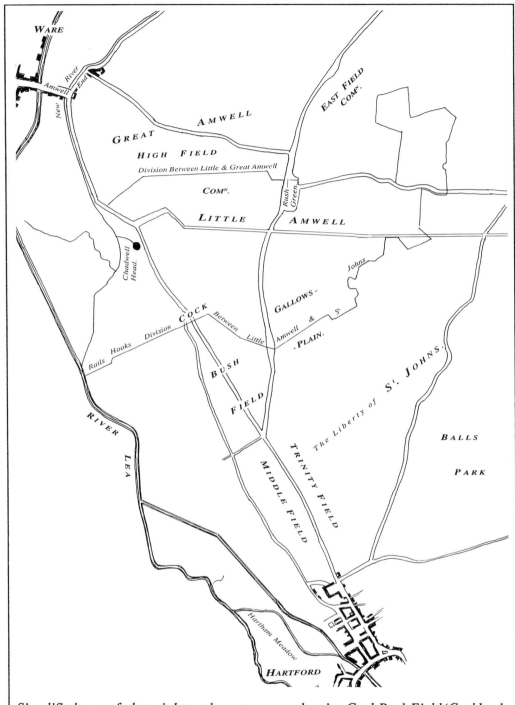

Simplified copy of a late eighteenth-century map showing Cock Bush Field (Corkbush Field) situated astride the road from Ware to Hertford. In the seventeenth century, it is probable that the road ran at a lower level to the north of Corkbush Field. (Based upon Hertfordshire Record Office: D/Ex 67 P. 1)

the Generals. They accused them of "obstructing and opposing our proceedings", believing they had obtained an agreement for virtual manhood suffrage (excluding servants and beggars) only to find the Generals denied this and also disclaimed any agreement to hold a general rendezvous. Lilburne's influence over the situation was considerable, though some of the new agents may well have been acting independently. Although the message repeated again in the pamphlet was for all to attend a General Rendezvous, there was not enough time for Lilburne to get all those regiments sympathetic to his cause to Ware on time. However, the message had gone out that as far as the Levellers and new agents were concerned, the rendezvous at Corkbush Field was "that we may all agree together in fulfilling our Declarations and Engagements to the people" and "all resolve to meet and not to part untill the rights and freedoms of us all and of all our countrey-men be settled and secured". Fairfax and Cromwell, however, had other plans for Corkbush Field.

Corkbush Field

Where was Corkbush Field and why was it chosen? It was the name given to land to the east of Hertford along the Ware road, lying between the Meads at the bottom of the valley of the River Lea and the higher ground to the south known as Barrow Green Common. On a map drawn 100 years later, Corkbush Field is seen running for over half a mile on either side of the Ware road from the point where a track led to Rush Green to just west of the Chadwell Spring, then the source of the New River. Part of this road probably ran at a lower level than it now does. The headquarters was established in Hertford and the regiments were able to camp out in the Meads and along the escarpment to Ware. Horses would have had fodder in the Meads and the fresh water from the New River. Whether or not any consideration was given to the north-facing aspect is unknown, but if a strong east wind was blowing, the regiments would have been unwilling to spend too long standing still in the open and exposed to the elements. Fairfax may well have got his way if this was the case. Given that the army had spent considerable time previously within the county, the Generals had probably noted it as an ideal spot for a future rendezvous. The location, in an area which they felt able to control, gave them the opportunity to enforce discipline through persuading rank-and-file soldiers to accept a new set of documents. These included a *Remonstrance to the Soldiers*, which the Generals claimed to have prepared with the Army Council, a *Declaration*, which was a set of resolutions in Fairfax's name, and a form agreeing to army discipline to which the soldiers had to subscribe.

Corkbush Field today — it extended from the junction with Gallows Hill almost to the flyover of the A10 in the distance. Cockbush Avenue (right) would have been in the middle of the field.

The Remonstrance to the Soldiers

It is clear from the wording of these documents that they were designed both to enforce discipline but also to hold out considerable hope that the soldiers' demands would be met. They were probably a joint effort by the senior officers, with Fairfax, Cromwell and Ireton all having a part in their composition. The fact that all the soldiers present, through their officers, agreed to the new declaration is probably of far greater importance than the death of Private Arnold. In the *Remonstrance* the Generals justified their actions over the previous few months and claimed they were still open to any sober suggestion to secure the future. They specifically attacked the activities of the new agents — the recently elected Leveller agitators who had replaced the old ones — as acting under the influence of 'private persons' who were not of the army, and as attacking the integrity of the general officers and council. They accused the new agents of making factions, discontents and mutinies in the army and undermining its discipline, as well as creating a delay to its proceedings. This was clearly an attack on the civilian Levellers, in particular on Lilburne, Wildman and those who had argued for days at Putney about the *Agreement*. The reference to mutinies, presumably refers to the moving mutinies at St. Albans, Luton and Dunstable and other incidents such as those mentioned above, as well as the arrival against orders of the two regiments. Clearly the generals were not going to recognise the new agents as true representatives and may well have seized on them as being convenient scapegoats.

Fairfax's then set out in the *Remonstrance* his justification for calling three separate rendezvous. He said he had decided to send the officers and agitators from Putney back to their regiments not only to compose the discontents and divisions that had arisen in them, but also to ease the country people of the burden of free quarter. He said the Generals had drawn together those regiments who were already quartered in the area, and there was no other reason than that for calling those particular regiments to Corkbush Field. However he blamed the new agents for persuading other regiments to turn up "in a disorderly and confused manner to the oppression of the country and disaccommodation (if not quarrelling and destruction) of the soldiery in quartering." He then threatened to resign if these "abuses and disorders" continued. Fairfax therefore saw the rendezvous as the occasion for a showdown with the Levellers and their sympathisers, hoping to isolate them and brand them as acting against the interests of the army and in favour of their own deluded schemes.

4
15th November 1647

The seven regiments

Having explained why the rendezvous took place at Corkbush Field and what were the expectations of the various groups present, we now turn to what happened on the day. There are a number of accounts — official, semi-official, partial and those embodied in statements made later which were self-justificatory — and they often appear to contradict one another. The exact sequence of events therefore is not easy to disentangle. First, there is Fairfax's letter sent from Hertford on the evening of the 15th November to the Earl of Manchester, as Speaker of the House of Lords, which gives the General's immediate views on what had taken place. Secondly there is an official version printed by Gilbert Mabbot and signed by William Clarke, Clerk to the Army Council, also dated 15th November. Then there are various newspaper reports from the time, reported speeches of others such as Cromwell in Parliament, comments on the events in other tracts and pamphlets, and the later printed recollections of Leveller sympathisers such as Captain-Lieutenant Bray.

In some accounts it appears that all the regiments, including those that were there against orders, were assembled on the field before Fairfax's arrival. It was the designated rendezvous for seven regiments of the New Model Army including the horse regiments of Fairfax, and Colonels Riche, Fleetwood and Twistleton, and the foot regiments of Fairfax, and Colonels Pride and Hammond. As far as the Generals were concerned neither Lilburne's foot regiment nor Colonel Thomas Harrison's horse regiment should have come to Corkbush Field. However the most recent account by Ian Gentles in his book, *The New Model Army*, suggests that only the seven regiments authorised to attend were present at the start of proceedings, but that they were already being encouraged to sign the *Agreement* by officers not holding commissions in the New Model Army. Later Harrison's regiment turned up uninvited, and later still Colonel Robert Lilburne's. One newspaper report said that others had set out to come but had then gone back to their billets. The following day a news-sheet reported that a soldier called Allin (Joseph Aleyn, a recently elected new agent) was responsible for persuading others in Harrison's regiment to attend. Some of the soldiers in Lilburne's and Harrison's regiments had copies of the *Agreement* stuck in their hatbands.

Before the arrival of the two regiments, however, two events had taken place. First, Colonel Rainsborough presented *An Agreement of the People* with the *Humble Petition from the Soldiers* to Fairfax as soon as he appeared on the field. Then Major Thomas Scott, Colonel William Eyre (or Eyres) and others, including Major John Cobbett, encouraged the soldiers to stand by the principles contained in the *Agreement*. Cobbett had been the sole representative at the Putney Debates for Skippon's Regiment, which was waiting in Newcastle to be relieved by Robert Lilburne's Regiment. Cobbett had opposed some of the resolutions put to the officers' committee at Putney, and had sided with the Levellers two weeks before. Thomas Prince and Samuel Chidley, who were later arrested as being the 'London agents' responsible, said that all that was intended was "a peaceable proposing of the same petition to the soldiers for their concurrence". Major Scott was described by Fairfax as behaving "very factiously" and "not only testifying his own discontent but stirring up others to the same". The implication is that they had recently printed copies of the *Agreement* and had been trying to persuade others to put it in their hats. Fairfax then dealt with those who had been distributing the pamphlets, Eyre and others, presumably including Cobbett, being seized and put into the custody of the Provost Marshall. Major Scott was arrested and put under the guard of Lieutenant Chillendon and, as an M.P., sent to London to answer to Parliament. Rainsborough was also an M.P. but no action seems to have been taken against him at the time, though later he was given a commission in the navy. Other "inferior persons" were arrested, according to the official account, for distributing "sundry scandalous and factious papers" such as the *Agreement*.

The mutinous regiments

Having dealt with the Leveller agitators and officers who had attempted to subvert the seven regiments authorised to attend, Fairfax then turned to the first of the two regiments present against orders. This was Colonel Thomas Harrison's regiment of horse, though he himself was not present. The regiment had been quartered around Hertford in the winter of 1644-5 so were familiar with the area. Harrison had been involved in drawing up the proposals of the army in July, but did not feature in reports of the Putney Debates until the 9th November when he was listed as being on a committee drawing up a summary of the army's engagements and declarations. On the 11th November, at the second meeting of the committee, he was reported as saying that:

> The Kinge was a Man of Bloud, and therefore the Engagement taken off, and that they were to prosecute him. That if the Lords had right to

Foot regiments in both the parliamentary and royalist armies were made up of musketeers and pikemen. The pikemen were employed in close fighting between the infantry and to repel enemy cavalry. Their weapon was the pike, made from an ash stave of generally 16 feet in length with a steel head. Pikemen on both sides continued to wear armour -- this example having been made by a member of the Armourers' Company of London in about 1635. (The Board of Trustees of the Royal Armouries)

Musketeers outnumbered pikemen in the foot regiments by about two to one. They carried muskets, with musket rests for firing, and the remainder of their shooting equipment was suspended from a bandolier slung over the left shoulder. From the right shoulder was suspended a "baldrick" from which hung a sword, used in hand-to-hand fighting. However, in many of the battles of the Civil War the infantry made more effective use of their musket butts, wielding their firearms as clubs, than they did of their swords. (The Board of Trustees of the Royal Armouries)

have a Negative voice hee would nott goe against it, butt iff nott, if they had usurp't [it] an 100, 200 or 1000 yeares, the greater was the wronge, and they to bee debarr'd of that power.

He was answered by Cromwell, Ireton and Fairfax, who all argued against the idea that the army should bring the King to trial independently of Parliament. Thus Harrison had already adopted one of the key Leveller demands, and testimony six years later by a Lieutenant Rockwell implied that Harrison had gone further than this. Colonel Reynolds, to whose regiment Rockwell had been transferred, claimed in a letter to Cromwell in 1653 that Rockwell had told him "that he was on[e] of those that whore papers in his hatt wrighten with cappital letters Englands Freedom and Souldiers Rights, when your Lordship was at Ware". This however was denied by Rockwell in a subsequent interview, but he did not deny "that Major General Harrison did at that tyme side with the souldiery" and he agreed that he said that Harrison had deserted the General because of the proposed treaty with the King. Even though this evidence is second-hand, it does fit in with Harrison's statements at Putney, suggesting both that Harrison was sympathetic to the soldiers and that Cromwell was definitely at Corkbush Field.

The exact role of Cromwell in these proceedings is still open to doubt. The official version mentions him only as responding to soldiers in Lilburne's regiment when they cried out that they had been abused by their officers. Cromwell said that they should have justice against them. Other reports tell of him trying to rip the papers from the hats of Harrison's regiment as they had arrived without their officers and had no one to discipline them. Realising that the other regiments present were not going to go along with them, they removed the papers themselves and agreed to obey Fairfax.

The doubt about Cromwell's role has been raised by Mark Kishlansky who in an article *"What Happened at Ware?"* argues that Cromwell was not present at all. This is because he dismisses the accounts in the royalist news-sheets and secret correspondence, which report the subsequently much quoted incident when Cromwell charged sword in hand into the ranks of Lilburne's regiment to restore order. Subsequent to Kishlansky's article, a number of historians, notably Austin Woolrych, have argued that Cromwell was present and the incident with Harrison's regiment probably did take place.

Having cowed the firebrands in Harrison's regiment, Fairfax decided to review all the troops on the field. He went to the head of each regiment where the *Remonstrance* was read and the soldiers were persuaded to subscribe to it. Apparently most did this quite willingly. The reason for this was that the Grandees had made considerable concessions to the Leveller viewpoint in the Committee of the Army Council which had drawn up the document. For example, they had agreed to press for the soldiers' professional grievances over pay and arrears, indemnity for acts committed during the war and provision for widows and orphans. They also made important political concessions. These included an agreement that a limit should be put to the time that the Long Parliament should remain in session. It had been sitting since 1640 and new elections were long overdue. The most significant concession was over the wording of the details on how elections should be conducted. Not only were elections to be regular and on fixed days, as the *Agreement* had originally suggested, but "for the freedom and equality of elections thereto, to render the House of Commons (as near as may be) an equal representative of the people that are to elect." Though this was sufficiently vague to be open to a variety of interpretations, it appeared to include phrases with which some Leveller sympathisers would be happy. Whether or not the Grandees were cynically playing with words in order to re-assert their authority is a possibility, but to many it looked like a commitment to new elections and a more representative Parliament. In the circumstances it worked and the soldiers subscribed.

Half-way through this process the second regiment to attend against orders turned up. This was Robert Lilburne's foot regiment which had come from St. Albans, 16 miles away across the county. They must have been marching for most of the day and, like Harrison's regiment, wore printed copies of the *Agreement* in their hats. They were commanded to take them out, which they initially refused to do, and Captain-Lieutenant Bray, the most senior officer left with them, was arrested to be tried later.

An incident is then reported by Rushworth that indicates the extent to which the mutineers were prepared to go. Major George Gregson, of Colonel Thomas Pride's regiment, which was apparently drawn up next to the new arrivals, harangued the mutineers and shouted at them to submit to military discipline. An ordinary soldier, Bartholomew Symonds, responded by proclaiming that the Major was 'against the King'. This resulted in others throwing stones at Gregson and injuring his head. Meanwhile Fairfax had been continuing with his review of the other troops. He finally came to Lilburne's regiment, by which time Henry Lilburne and some of the junior officers had arrived, remarking later of their troops that they "stood with white papers in their hats, as if they had been going to engage with an enemy".

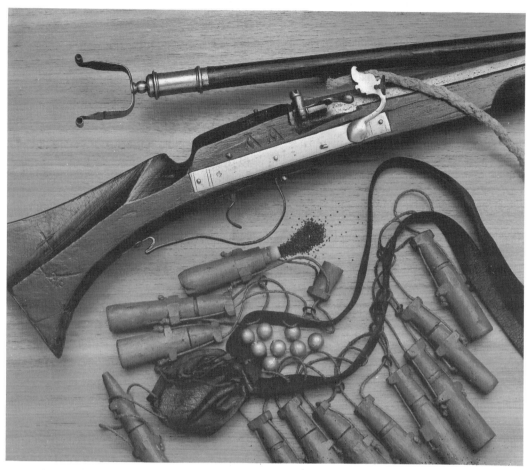

A matchlock musket, as used by foot regiments of the New Model Army, with a musket rest and bandolier. The musket, from the Littlecote House armoury, is one of the few examples struck with the Commons and Lords mark introduced in 1643/4. The wooden containers, which hung from the bandolier, each held enough gunpowder for a single shot. The piece of slow match held in the jaws of the musket's "serpentine" is an original 17th century example from the arsenal at Emden. The musket balls are modern castings. During the Civil War, the matchlock musket was more common than the more efficient (and expensive) flintlock. (The Board of Trustees of the Royal Armouries – objects XII 5347, XIII 93, XIII 917, XII 930)

The role of Oliver Cromwell

Fairfax apparently ordered the men to take the papers from their hats and, on their refusal to do so, he asked Henry Lilburne and his officers to point out the ringleaders. Then some of his officers moved forward and removed the papers and, according to royalist sources, Cromwell was foremost in doing so. Given that Cromwell had consistently opposed the Leveller demands in the Army Council and had the reputation for acting rapidly and decisively when he was convinced he was right, this action would be in character. It would be appropriate that a senior officer, other than Fairfax, should actually carry out the key confrontation with the mutineers. This bold move seemed to have worked and order was restored. Things however could not rest there. The ringleaders of the moving mutinies at St. Albans, Luton and Dunstable had not yet been brought to justice. In one incident an officer had lost his hand and two soldiers had been killed. Retribution had to be sought. Eleven mutineers were then seized from the ranks, subjected to court-martial, found guilty of mutiny and sentenced to death. However Fairfax decided to commute the sentence on all but three — for what reason has never been made clear. Maybe this was because three soldiers had been killed or injured at Dunstable and confirming the sentence on an equal number was seen as just retribution. The three remaining had to cast lots for their lives. Richard Arnold lost and was then shot by the other two in front of his fellow soldiers. Henry Lilburne later commented:

> And I well remember some of the Officers of that Regiment did much rejoyce in the just hand of God, directing the Lot upon that man, whom they had observed to be more notoriously guilty than any other in this business.

Fairfax was clearly making a public example of one man, who may or may not have been guilty of actually starting the mutiny. The fact that the Grandees could effectively punish a series of mutinies and prevent the development of an even greater one by judicially executing one man says a great deal for army discipline and the hold that the senior officers had over their men.

It was clearly Fairfax, not Cromwell who ordered the court-martial and the sentences and execution. Cromwell's role was as the second-in-command, the hard man of action, whose duty was to quell any nascent mutiny. Royalist letters of intelligence suggested that Cromwell himself was under threat of being arrested for treason and had to make a show of force against the

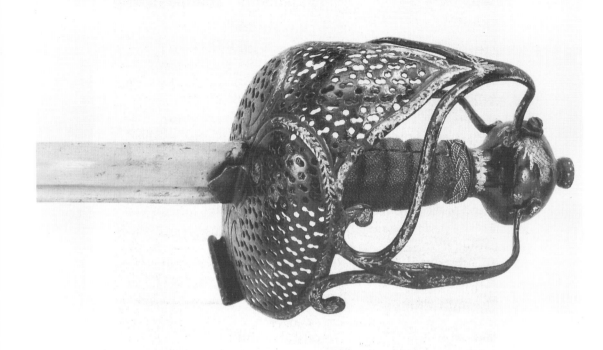

Cromwell's sword: the sword traditionally carried by Oliver Cromwell at the taking of Drogheda in 1649. (The Board of Trustees of the Royal Armouries — object IX 1096)

Levellers. They report him as deporting himself "very gallantly and prudently" at the rendezvous and that "coming to the head of the regiment, [he] drew his sword and charged so furiously through it, as the regiment, (being much astonished therewith), pulled out their whites [papers] and craved mercy." After charging in he is reported to have "wheeled about and changing his countenance spake fairly to them demanding what they would have." Although we may question the truth of these reports some of these actions seem typical of Cromwell. Certainly one outcome of the Ware Mutiny was that both Fairfax's and Cromwell's reputations were enhanced with groups and factions other than the Levellers. Woolrych records how four days later, when Cromwell gave his own account to the Commons, they voted him thanks "for his good service to the Parliament and Kingdom, at the late Rendezvous of the Army" and comments that, since they had already thanked Fairfax, the implication was that Cromwell had performed a signal act that called for special recognition. This view is supported by the *Perfect Weekly Account* for

Oliver Cromwell by Sir Peter Lely — the protrait in which he asked to be painted "warts and all"   (Cromwell Museum, Huntingdon)

the 19th November, which recorded the same episode in the Commons who "ordered that the Lieutenant-Gen. and all the officers of the Army which were active in allaying mutinies in the Army, should have the thanks of the house". Even before the Ware Mutiny, Cromwell had been referred to in royalist pamphlets as "King Oliver" and exaggerated accounts of his role and this recognition by Parliament only confirmed suspicions about his ambition.

The pacification of the army

The Ware Mutiny of the 15th November thus has to be seen as both the culmination of a series of mutinies and disturbances in the army, largely over pay, and also the result of a radical political movement originating in London to change the constitution of the country.   Mutinies had taken place in companies of Robert Lilburne's Regiment when they were passing through St. Albans, Luton and Dunstable.   Fairfax's own regiment of foot had been involved in mutinous disturbances at Ware eleven days before, and Ireton's and Harrison's regiments were likewise affected.   The attack on Major Gregson at Ware was itself a form of mutiny, as were the attempts by Eyre and Cobbett to influence soldiers in other regiments.   At Ware these stirrings of mutiny were not able to spread because the Grandees now had the situation under control, whereas they were not present during previous disturbances and therefore had been unable to assert their authority.

One outcome of the mutinies was that Private Arnold was shot.   Another was that a number of other mutineers, along with those previously arrested on the day, were held for trial at a later date.   The accounts of 1647-8 for the third mayoralty of Ralphe Pollard in St. Albans Borough indicate that ten mutineers from Lilburne's regiment were brought from Hertford to the gaol at St. Albans. These with Arnold would have made up the 11 ringleaders arrested at Corkbush Field.   The mayor then paid out eight shillings for timber to make a wooden horse, presumably for the punishment and cashiering of the soldiers. A later account of a similar punishment in March 1649 indicates what would have happened : "Sentenced to ride the horse, with their faces to the taile, their swords broke over their heads, and to be cashiered the army".   However some of them became sick and the mayor had to pay out further sums for them and their guards who occupied the house of one Alban Spencer.   Meanwhile Fairfax had moved to Ruislip Heath to the second rendezvous.   It would therefore make sense to incarcerate the mutineers on the way, neither leaving them at Ware nor taking them to Watford where they might become an object of other soldiers' sympathy.   Fairfax was confident that the local committee in Hertfordshire would back him.   Thus, those men from Robert Lilburne's regiment who had been left unpunished after Corkbush Field seem to have been cashiered at St. Albans, the location of their initial mutiny, while the fomenters of mutiny at Ware were being taken to the army's headquarters at Windsor.

The second rendezvous saw the review of only three groups of soldiers,

Okey's dragoons and Waller's and Lambert's regiments of foot. The third rendezvous a day later on the Hare Warren near Kingston went off equally peaceably. There a larger number of soldiers were drawn up including those from regiments led by Ireton, Waller, Barkstead, Overton and Hewson as well as the General's lifeguard and those in Rainsborough's former regiment, now under the command of Colonel Richard Deane. In three days over 17 regiments had been reviewed and had agreed to the *Remonstrance* and the accompanying documents. This did not include some of the more troublesome regiments which were stationed some distance from the capital, though support for Fairfax did come in from others. On the day of the third rendezvous letters of support came from Sir Hardress Waller's regiment in which they attacked "the disorderly actings derogatory from the command of your excellency, whereby the united composure of this army is somewhat disjointed." Three companies of Okey's dragoons, which were stationed in Lincolnshire, later said they would live and die with Fairfax and would not "adhere in the least to the counsels and practices of these surreptitious Agents, who under the pretence of Freedom, would freely and willingly captivate us to their Anarchical Liberty". Eleven days after Corkbush Field, Colonel Robert Lilburne and his officers wrote apologising for their failure to control their men and decrying the "distractions and distempers in the army". However although they said they were the first to "taste of those dangers", they asked Fairfax to continue pressing on with the army's solemn engagements.

5

The Results of the Mutiny

The immediate results of the activities at Corkbush Field were threefold. First, the Generals' position as against the Parliament, the Scots and the King was strengthened since they were no longer seen as leading a divided army. Secondly, they could now rely on the loyalty of the vast majority of their troops and were able to threaten to send a regiment into London in order to secure the army's pay. Thirdly, they were able to play the Parliament off against the Levellers and use Parliament's fear of radical change to court-martial other Leveller ringleaders. The suppression of the mutiny had little impact on their immediate dealings with the King and the Scots. In the long run, however, it may have contributed to bringing the King and the Scots together, since both now feared that a united army dominated by senior officers of an Independent persuasion and middle-rank officers, many of whom were Baptists and millenarians, was a much greater danger than one controlled by a Presbyterian-dominated Parliament.

Parliamentary reaction

The effect on Parliament is seen almost instantly. Colonel Rainsborough was summoned to attend the House of Commons and a letter sent to Fairfax thanking him for "his reducing the mutineers and settling the army." They also appointed a committee to inquire into what meetings had been taking place among the 'London Agents' which had led to the 'dividing of the army' and Scott and Rainsborough were ordered to answer for their actions to it. The Commons agreed to consider providing money for the army on the Thursday and as a result the Treasurers at War were told to send ready cash "towards the making up of a month's pay." A joint committee of both houses was also set up to investigate the authors of "these seditious irregularities."

On the 19th November Cromwell gave the House of Commons his account of the proceedings at all three rendezvous and he was asked to inform Fairfax that the Commons would always be ready to receive any "humble addresses as shall be made from the Army." Later that day, however, Fairfax sent a letter to the chairman of the Commons' Army Committee indicating that he had given orders for Colonel Hewson's foot regiment to march into and quarter in the City of London to aid in the "service of bringing in the arrears upon the city." The message was clear. Unless the City paid up, they would have the army taking free quarter on their citizens. On the next day, Cromwell was asked to order Hewson's regiment to hold back from the City and a committee of both houses was established to put pressure on the City authorities to pay up.

News on the 23rd November of another mutiny at Bristol three days before — when soldiers had seized a local alderman and refused to release him unless a month's pay was provided — led to a resolution in the Commons that for the following fortnight provision for the army and free quarter would take priority. Meanwhile the Lords had received information that on the 17th *An Agreement of the People* had been distributed from an inn in Friday Street in the City called the Saracen's Head and that letters had been sent out as far as Nottingham to get people to subscribe to it. This appears to have led to an investigation in the City as by the 23rd it was ordered that Thomas Prince, a cheesemonger, and Samuel Chidley were being imprisoned in the Gatehouse and that Jeremy Ives, Thomas Taylor and William Larner were being committed to Newgate for distributing the *Agreement*. Fairfax was then thanked for his suppression of the mutineers and encouraged to punish any others in the army who were found guilty.

The fate of the accused

How many in the army and elsewhere were punished as a result of the mutiny is difficult to disentangle from the pamphlet warfare that subsequently went on. It is clear that Scott and Rainsborough were investigated, and that Rainsborough's naval appointment was held up as a result. Scott however appeared to have got off 'Scott free'. Subsequent pamphlets issued by Prince and Chidley and by Bray indicate some of the consequences, though they have to be read with circumspection. On 28th November eight men held prisoner by the Marshall-General petitioned Fairfax. These included Bray, Eyre, John Wood, William Thompson, John Crosman, William Pryor, George Hassall and Thomas Beverley. William Everard may also have signed it later. Their petition was a direct attack on Henry Lilburne, Robert Lilburne's younger brother and a junior officer in his own regiment, whom they wanted investigated. However it is not clear whether they were all present at the Ware Mutiny or just happened to be in prison together.

On the 3rd December, a Council of War was held at Windsor which tried various men from Lilburne's regiment. This was not a General Council of the Army with the elected agents present, but a court-martial run by the Grandees.

As a result six or seven of the accused were sentenced to run the gauntlet, a punishment which was carried out the next day. A corporal had also been sentenced to be executed, apparently for being involved in the deaths in the "former mutiny". This may have been decided on as only Arnold had been shot and two deaths at Luton required another to be executed. Sentence however was postponed until Bray's full trial and that of the "ringleaders of the mutinous party". Captain-Lieutenant Bray had been brought in but "carried himself with that pride and arrogancy that was a scandal to all honest men". A further trial was held on Wednesday 15th December at Windsor of those involved in the actual resistance at Ware. Bartholomew Symonds was condemned to die because he had led the attack on Major Gregson, being described as "the chief ringleader of the Mutiny at the rendezvous neer Ware". Another soldier called Bell was condemned to run the gauntlet twice for being active in the mutiny.

Bray and Cobbett were also put on trial and, by midnight on the 20th December, the court had agreed that Cobbett should be cashiered but that the General Council of the Army should have the final decision. However here the Grandees' actions received a check. Captain-Lieutenant John Ingram of General Fairfax's lifeguard, a junior officer of the same rank as Bray, intervened and queried whether the court could pass such a sentence. He himself was threatened with being cashiered, but the intervention seems to have had an important effect for when the General Council met again on the 23rd December the mood had changed. Ingram wrote to Fairfax on the evening of the 21st saying that he would obey Fairfax as long as Fairfax acted according to the "publique declarations of the whole soldiery at Triplowe Heath for Justice" and according to the *Solemn Engagement of the Army* made at Thriplow Heath, near Newmarket. Although Bray had been charged with acting contrary to orders and tried by the Council of War, on the 23rd December he and Crosman acknowledged their "rash and irregular proceedings" and agreed to submit to army discipline. They were then released and enabled to re-join their regiments, but Bray proceeded to publish a pamphlet in January 1648 justifying his previous actions. He quarrelled with his Colonel, Robert Lilburne, and was discharged. A maverick character, he raised soldiers in Kent to fight the royalists in the Second Civil War in 1648 but refused to join another's regiment when ordered to do so. He was again in trouble with the authorities and was imprisoned in Windsor for a personal attack of Fairfax. Later released, he was still writing Leveller tracts in 1659 in the months before the Restoration of Charles II.

John Cobbett had been a Major in Skippon's foot regiment and had represented his regiment, which was stationed at Newcastle, at the Army Council. His sentence of the 20th December to be cashiered appears to have been rescinded on the 23rd, when the Generals met in the last of three long prayer meetings, and decided to revoke the recent sentences passed on all the mutineers in order to bring about army unity. Ironically he helped to recapture Tynemouth Castle in the Second Civil War, following the defection to the royalists of Colonel Henry Lilburne. However, he then tried to persuade his regiment, when they were stationed at Bristol in May 1649, to join the Burford Mutiny and was again court-martialled and cashiered. However like Eyre, he was re-instated and fought at both the battles of Dunbar and Worcester, dying in 1657.

Colonel William Eyre, who was unconnected with the New Model Army, was like Bray a maverick character. He was later caught up in a scheme of Henry Marten, the republican, to raise irregular forces in August 1648 following the defeat of the royalists in the second civil war. Marten feared that Parliament was going to do a deal with the King so he and Eyre started to raise forces in Marten's home county of Berkshire. They obtained horses by breaking into gentlemen's stables and taking them from others passing on the highway. The House of Commons had then to use local forces to suppress them. In May 1649 Eyre joined the Leveller mutiny at Burford, was taken prisoner and released on a surety of £1,000. He appears to have eventually accepted army discipline as he fought against the Scots at Worcester.

John Wood was probably one of the two elected agents from Commissary-General Ireton's regiment of horse. William Thompson had been originally a corporal in Colonel Whalley's regiment, but was in trouble throughout 1647, being cashiered and later imprisoned in Windsor where he wrote a pamphlet entitled *England's Freedoms Soldiers' Rights*, possibly in collaboration with John Lilburne. He remained an active Leveller throughout 1648 and led a mutiny of the New Model Army at Banbury in May 1649, subsequently being hunted down and killed in Northamptonshire. His brother James and other rebels joined the related mutiny at Burford.

William Pryor, one of the original agitators from Fleetwood's regiment, and therefore probably present at Ware, appears also to have been pardoned but was later arrested in 1655 for plotting with other Levellers against Cromwell when he was Lord Protector. Of Hassall and Beverley no more is known. The effect on these men of the suppression of the Ware Mutiny and of the

John Lilburne at his trial in 1649 with the medal struck to commemorate his acquittal   (By permission of The British Library — "The Triall of Lieut. Collonell John Lilburne" illustration before title page)

subsequent leniency by the Army Council seems to have encouraged some to continue their activities even to death while others drifted back into obscurity or into more extreme forms of Leveller activity. By Christmas 1647, Lilburne's regiment was expected to replace Skippon's in the Newcastle garrison, thus fulfilling Fairfax's initial orders to them. The question then is raised did the Mutiny and its suppression achieve anything in either the short or long term?

The reaction of the Levellers

John Lilburne realising that he had failed to get acceptance of the *Agreement* had returned to the Tower from Ware. The royalist news-sheet *Mercurius Pragmaticus* proclaimed that, on hearing the news of Arnold's death, he "cry'd out Treason, Treason, give me my horse, which was no sooner brought him, but he mounted his palfrey, and rid like any beggar a horseback, till he came to his court at Bedlam". This was presumably journalistic fiction. The official account of the Ware Mutiny said merely that things had not succeeded to his expectation. However Lilburne was active in raising further petitions to Parliament and in demanding justice for the death of Arnold, who in the eyes of some became a martyr for the Leveller cause. On the 23rd November, Thomas Prince, Samuel Chidley, Captain Taylor, Mr. William Larner and Mr. Ives presented a petition to Parliament in which they gave their version of the events at Ware. They said that all that was done at Ware was "a peaceable proposing of the same petitions to the souldiery, for their concurrence" and the "just and peaceable persuance of Freedome". They especially requested that Parliament "make inquisition for the blood of that soldier viz. Richard Arnall, of Col. Lilburne's Regiment, which was shot to death neere Ware". The reaction of the Commons was to put Prince and Chidley in the Gatehouse prison and the others in Newgate for "seditious and contemptuous array and prosecuting of a former petition." These Levellers had also been accused of conspiring to assassinate the King, to which they had replied that Cromwell and Ireton had deliberately frightened the King into fleeing from Hampton Court, to get him away from Parliament and more completely in their power. Given the rapid and unexpected turn of events, it is not surprising that charge and counter charge were being made.

Sixteen months later, in a pamphlet entitled *The Second Part of England's New-Chaines Discovered* Lilburne said Arnold had been shot "for pursuing the ends of the Engagement at Newmarket and for insisting upon *An Agreement of the People*". Richard Overton developed the same theme in a pamphlet called *The Hunting of the Foxes from New-Market and Triploe-Heaths to Whitehall, By five small Beagles (late of the Armie)*, published in March 1649. Overton argued that Arnold "a private souldier was shot to death for promoting and assisting the work of the souldiers in reference to the Solemn Engagement of the Army". For Wildman and others, Arnold had died merely for supporting the soldiers' just rights and was therefore innocent : "O let that day never be forgotten! let not the bloud of that innocent person be here had out of remembrance, until justice be had for the same". However this attempt to create a martyr for a cause, which in 1649 was again perceived to be under threat of extinction from Cromwell, ignored any part Arnold may have played in the previous mutinies. We are unlikely to know any more details of his involvement in them, or in the Leveller activities at Ware. However the Levellers in subsequent petitions argued that he should never have been tried by court-martial but should have been subject to civilian legal processes. This was based on the notion that the troops were private citizens first and soldiers second. Fairfax and Cromwell necessarily maintained that as long as they remained soldiers they were subject to military discipline. The Leveller case was weakened in the Generals' eyes by their insistence that the regiments could not be dissolved before the payment of arrears, an implicit admittance that they were clearly still in army units, although not active ones.

As a result of the failure of the civilian Levellers to get the *Agreement* officially accepted, they tightened up their own organisation in London. They set up a central treasury under Prince and Chidley, collected subscriptions and signatures for a variety of new petitions and began to operate like a modern political pressure group. However their support was largely limited to the London area in the first instance. They continued to influence both the rank and file in some regiments, though less directly than before. The Levellers however also lost out in personal terms. The *Agreement* was never adopted, even though a modified version was discussed in later councils of the army. Lilburne spent much of the rest of his life in prison or in exile, having quarrelled with every regime since the 1630s.

The Levellers and the rank and file

Although the Levellers suffered a severe set back, what was the reaction within the rank and file to the incidents at Corkbush Field? The failure of the mutiny significantly reduced the influence of the civilian Levellers within the New Model Army. They had tried to use their ultimate weapon, direct action by the ordinary soldiers and junior officers against the Grandees, and it had failed. Having failed once it was going to be very difficult to attempt a widespread mutiny again. When it was tried again at London and then at Burford, the reaction of the Grandees was the same. At London, Lockyer was shot as the ringleader, and at Burford, where some men on both sides had already been lost in a skirmish through the streets, three Levellers were shot in the churchyard. It was clear to the Grandees that the bulk of the soldiers in the New Model Army were loyal to Fairfax and, when it came to making a choice, they were prepared to side with him and to oppose the Levellers.

This then raises two other related questions. Why did the other regiments remain loyal, and had the Levellers over-estimated their influence on the rank and file? The answer to the first, suggested by John Morrill in *The Nature of the English Revolution*, is that Parliament had already passed legislation to meet the main grievances of the soldiers over arrears of pay and indemnity. The problem was persuading the counties to pay for the arrears. This was slow to be implemented but depended on the exactly the opposite policy from that advocated by the Levellers. They wanted the abolition of the wartime committees, but the soldiers saw that the continuance of this bureaucracy was the only way they were going to get paid. In September and October Parliament appointed a new Committee of the Army with extensive powers to collect money from the local committees and efforts were made to get money from the City of London. They also set up an Indemnity Committee which by August was already beginning to protect soldiers from those trying to prosecute them. The Ware Mutiny therefore perhaps came too late, as the soldiers could see that the existing structures were beginning to help them. They were not going to overthrow them just when they were proving beneficial.

The Levellers may have over-estimated their strength within the rank and file. The election of new agents, some of whom were not representative of the whole regiment, may have been resented by the soldiers. The *Agreement* was a reduced version of *The Case of the Army Truly Stated*, a pamphlet drawn up by these new agents. Many may have felt they were being steam-rollered into accepting a theoretical document, the contents of which they had neither contributed to nor understood. They wanted money and protection from prosecution and were not prepared to risk death for theories of which they were by nature suspicious. Many in the ranks of the New Model Army were conservative in their social views and had been brought up with habits of obedience, reinforced by army discipline. They did not see themselves as revolutionaries. Fairfax's *Remonstrance to the Soldiers* represented most of

The execution of Charles I in January 1649—from a German woodcut of the time. The executioner holds up the King's head while his soul is received into Heaven by angels hovering above the Banqueting House in Whitehall.

what they wanted and when presented as the *Humble Representation* to Parliament in December, the means was found to implement it. The restricted nature of Leveller influence can be seen from the facts that there were no incidents at the two subsequent rendezvous, that the agitators were excluded from the meetings of the Army Council and that within two months 18,000 men of the New Model Army were quietly disbanded.

Effects on the direction of politics

However the Ware mutiny and its suppression had other important political side effects. The Presbyterians in Parliament and their Scots allies moved closer to an agreement with the King. They saw the Independents as creatures of the army, and the Grandees' apparently lenient treatment of the remaining mutineers may well have decided the Scots to clinch the secret deal with the King over Christmas. Although the Leveller leadership had apparently gained little, criticism by Wildman and Lilburne of the Generals for their dealings with the King may have had its effect. Once the King had rejected Parliament's attempts to settle the conditions for further negotiations on the 28th November, there was little point in the army continuing its own negotiations, given the attitude of the rank and file. By the end of 1647, the Grandees and parliamentary leaders met to consider their next moves and on the 3rd January 1648 it was agreed that the two houses would make no further addresses to the King, i.e. not attempt to enter into any personal treaty. The Grandees therefore were influenced by the ideas being put forward in the *Agreement*, and it is significant that later written constitutions produced by the Grandees contained key elements from the *Agreement* such as limited length to Parliaments, exclusion of the title 'King', etc.

Given that the Ware Mutiny was about soldiers' arrears and rights, what did they achieve in the end? Sir Thomas Dacres, the Hertfordshire M.P., was able to get a comprehensive bill through Parliament to help the widows and orphans of fallen soldiers, and the mass of petitions from individual parishes in Hertfordshire stating the amount of free quarter taken, do seem to have eventually borne fruit. Civilians received compensation, and soldiers received some back pay. They were also given debentures that related to confiscated land, which they could cash in, not just for land in England, but later for that confiscated in Ireland in the 1650s. It was the most loyal of Cromwell's supporters, such as the Baptist Lieutenant-Colonel Daniel Axtell, who not only led the guard at the King's trial but who was also later responsible for brutally suppressing the Irish. The army for Ireland was formed, but did not do its work until after the execution of the King. So was this first execution of Arnold justifiable? Cromwell thought so. He later told Edmund Ludlow that it was "absolutely necessary to keep things from falling into confusion; which must have ensued upon that division if it had not been timely prevented". Given the speed of events, perhaps Cromwell was right.

6
The Significance of the Mutiny

The Ware Mutiny was one of a series of dramatic events which happened so closely together that the main factions could not absorb or react to the significance of each one, before another dramatic event followed. Conspiracy theories necessarily develop when events flow so rapidly one upon another, even though they may be entirely disconnected. When the rate of change speeds up, but the channels of communication do not, then it is very difficult for those at the time and subsequently to assess the importance of events and any interconnections between them. For Cromwell, at that particular stage, the execution of Arnold was necessary. He saw the danger of division in the army leading to anarchy. The Ware Mutiny might have ended in anarchy if he had not intervened and if he and Fairfax had not decided to make an example of a soldier they believed had disobeyed orders and led a mutiny. The fact that they later refrained from executing any further soldiers indicates they saw that the immediate danger was over.

Views of Contemporaries —
Conspiracy or God's Providence?

Views at the time tended to centre around the role and position of Cromwell and the Levellers, as they still do today. A royalist correspondent of the King writing three days after the event said the Levellers had been disappointed by the turn of events and "now have very low thoughts of their cause, and it is believed they will scarce be able ever to gather head again". Sir Edward Hyde (later Earl of Clarendon) wrote a month later that

> No man can think that they who executed a leveller in the Head of the
> Regiment, and they who gave John Lilburne leave to walk London
> street the day before, intend one and the same thing.

In one respect both were right. The Levellers never had such a good chance again to influence the army and the event may have taken its particular form because there was little coherent co-operation between the Commons, who freed Lilburne, and the army who executed Arnold.

Cromwell in a speech to the Barebones Parliament in 1653 saw all the events of 1640s as the working of God's Providence, and hinted that perhaps the army and even he himself were Instruments of God in working out those providential 'necessities' on earth. In a speech to his first Protectorate Parliament a year later, he saw himself as having protected the natural magistracy, the gentry from attack and as having prevented the Levellers bringing in a bogus equality. "The natural magistracy of the nation, was it not almost trampled under foot by men of levelling principles? ... For the orders of men and ranks of men, did not that levelling principle tend to the reducing of all to an equality?" Cromwell's critics however saw it in a different light. The conservative Denzil Holles in his memoirs saw the Ware Mutiny as part of a general conspiracy led by Cromwell to get supreme power. He saw "Mr. Cromwell and his Cabinet Council" as having conspired to give the King the impression that the Levellers were threatening him and had then shot the Leveller "to make up the disguise". They had encouraged Charles to flee to the Isle of Wight, having made sure that the Governor Hammond was aware in advance of what was happening. The radical republican Edmund Ludlow in his memoirs put Cromwell in a similar conspiratorial role:

> Cromwell, not contenting himself with his part in an equal government, puffed up by his successes to an expectation of greater things, and having done a bargain with the grandees in the house, either to comply with the King, or to settle things in a factious way without him, procured a party to stand by him in the seizing of some of those who appeared at the rendezvous in opposition to his designs.

For both these critics, writing after the event with the benefit of hindsight, a conspiracy by Cromwell and his supporters seemed an obvious explanation, given his subsequent rise to power. However both explanations ignore the role of Fairfax and the quiescence of the rest of the army, and the fact that Cromwell became the servant of the Republic in fighting its enemies in the early 1650s. Confusion and chaos is a more likely explanation for many of these events rather than Cromwellian conspiracy.

Modern views —
Order Restored or Revolution Defeated?

How have subsequent historians viewed the significance of the Ware Mutiny, and do these interpretations need to be modified in the light of the assembled evidence? It has been called "an indisciplined demonstration ... that went off at half cock", it has been viewed as a mutiny that never took place and it has been seen as part of a cunning plan by Cromwell. Given the unprecedented and volatile situation that existed in England between June and December 1647, it must have seemed to many that anything was possible. A king had been defeated and an army had become independent of its employer, Parliament. That army was divided in many different ways but also became united in its distrust of King, Parliament and the Scots. In the light of subsequent events — the Second Civil War, the purge of Parliament, the trial and execution of the King, the establishment of the republic, the defeat of both the Scots and Irish by Cromwell, and then his coming to power as Lord Protector in 1653 — the Ware Mutiny seems at the same time both an insignificant event and yet a key turning point.

One view held by left-wing historians is that at Corkbush Field revolution from below was checked. However this assumes that revolution was a real possibility and that it came from below. Revolution was not understood in the modern sense in the 17th century. It was not seen as the overthrow of the ruling class by the masses but as a complete cycle of movement in the Aristotelian sense, in that one form of government decayed and gave way to another and eventually returned to the first form. In fact this is what happened. There was a complete revolution, the Monarchy being overthrown and various other regimes being set up and then the Monarchy restored in 1660. The Ware Mutiny was not a Marxist revolution from below, but a political protest by middle-rank officers, inspired by middle-rank civilians and ex-army activists like Lilburne, and temporarily supported by a few within two regiments, whose first concern was their professional grievances, not political ideology.

If not a revolution, was it all a tragic mistake and misunderstanding or was it a genuine difference of interpretation over certain key concepts? One constant feature of the arguments that continued among the participants was over what was meant by 'dividing the army'. All in the army accepted that in the *Solemn Engagement*, agreed at Newmarket and Thriplow Heath in June, they had decided not to divide the army. This could be interpreted in a number of different ways. Grandees and Levellers both agreed this meant that no part of the army should be disbanded or reformed into new regiments for Ireland by Parliament until their arrears had been paid. However, having had two rendezvous at Newmarket and Thriplow Heath, where they agreed not to divide, the Levellers also interpreted this as meaning that the army should not be convened in separate rendezvous, but only in one general rendezvous. Thus when the three rendezvous were called they accused the Generals of dividing the army. The Grandees did not see this physical division of the army for purely military purposes as 'dividing the army' in the sense that they interpreted the *Solemn Engagement*. They likewise accused the Levellers of dividing the army when they sponsored the election of the new agents and of attempting to divide the army ideologically by trying to impose on it a political document, *An Agreement of the People*, when the army should have been concerned with uniting to protect its own professional interests.

As well as differences of interpretation over physical or ideological 'division', there was clearly an underlying reluctance among the Grandees to be seen to be continually challenging the political system. The *Agreement* was a direct challenge to all the previous constitutional arrangements, and the Grandees were not going to have a new written constitution forced on them at this stage. Even though Cromwell was later to adopt the idea, he and Fairfax were still in the autumn of 1647 attempting to produce a compromise modification of the existing system. It would take another year before they decided that the existing system had to change dramatically and that the King would have to be put on trial. Thus, although the Ware Mutiny could be seen as a check to potential revolution, those resisting change were themselves influenced sufficiently by the views of the Levellers and by subsequent events to carry out their own *coup d'état*. A year later the army put the King on trial and in 1649 they executed him. However before that the King was to lose a second civil war, a war which strengthened Cromwell and led to a further purging of Parliament. It was the subsequent disillusion with the King rather than the principles contained in the *Agreement* that led to the abolition of the Monarchy. The Ware Mutiny and its suppression prevented further mass Leveller infiltration of the army but, by strengthening the position of the Grandees, it also helped to make possible the army's own seizure of power after the Second Civil War. Thus, although in 1647 successful revolution from below was unlikely, order was restored in the army. The discipline imposed then helped some of the Grandees to carry out their own political revolution and themselves bring about two key demands of the Levellers, the removal of the King and the establishment of a written constitution. Though order in the army was largely restored, popular disturbances at Canterbury and elsewhere over the suppression of traditional Christmas celebrations presaged the disturbances in Kent that led to the Second Civil War. They also provided the opportunity for the Levellers to raise a further mutiny at Burford and elsewhere in 1649, the suppression of which proved far more bloody than the death of Private Arnold at Ware.

Army

21

AN
AGREEMENT
OF THE
PEOPLE

FOR

A firme and prefent Peace , upon
grounds of common-right and freedome ;

As it was propofed by the Agents of the five
Regiments of Horfe ; and fince by the generall approbation of the Army, offered to the joynt concurrence of all the free COMMONS of
ENGLAND.

The Names of the Regiments which have already appeared for the
Cafe, of *The Cafe of the Army truly ftated*, and for this
prefent Agreement, *VIZ.*

1. *Gen. Regiment.*	1. *Gen. Regiment.*
2. *Life-Guard.*	2. *Col. Sir Hardreffe*
3. *Lieut. Gen. Regiment.*	*Wallers Reg.*
4. *Com. Gen. Regiment,*	3. *Col. Lamberts Reg.*
5. *Col. Whaleyes Reg.* Of Horfe	4. *Col. Rairfboroughs* Of Foot,
6. *Col. Rickes Reg.*	*Regiment.*
7. *Col. Fleetwoods Reg.*	5. *Col. Overtons Rog.*
8. *Col. Harrifons Reg.*	6. *Col. Lilburns Reg.*
9. *Col. Twifldens Reg.*	7. *Col. Backfters Reg.*

Nou: 3 Printed *Anno Dom.* 1647.

Appendix I

AN AGREEMENT OF THE PEOPLE FOR
a firme and present Peace, upon grounds of
common-right and freedome;

As it was proposed by the Agents of the five Regiments of Horse; and since by the general approbation of the Army, offered to the joynt concurrence of all the free COMMONS of ENGLAND.

The Names of the Regiments which have already appeared for the Case, of *The Case of the Army truly stated*, and for this present Agreement, *VIZ.*

1. *Gen. Regiment.*	}	1. *Gen. Regiment.*	}	
2. *Life-Guard.*	}	2. *Col. Sir Hardresse*		
3. *Lieut. Gen. Regiment.*	}	*Wallers Reg.*	}	
4. *Com. Gen. Regiment.*	}	3. *Col. Lamberts Reg.*	}	
5. *Col. Whaleyes Reg.*	}	4. *Col. Rainsboroughs*		
6. *Col. Riches Reg.*	} Of Horse	*Regiment.*	} Of Foot	
7. *Col. Fleetwoods Reg.*	}	5. *Col. Overtons Reg.*	}	
8. *Col. Harrisons Reg.*	}	6. *Col. Lilburns Reg.*	}	
9. *Col. Twisdens Reg.*	}	7. *Col. Backsters Reg.*	}	

Printed *Anno Dom.* 1647.

An Agreement of the People, for a firme and present Peace, upon grounds of Common Right.

Having by our late labours and hazards made it appeare to the world at how high a rate wee value our just freedome, and God having so far owned our cause, as to deliver the Enemies thereof into our hands : We do now hold ourselves bound in mutual duty to each other, to take the best care we can for the future, to avoid both the danger of returning into a slavish condition, and the chargable remedy of another war : for as it cannot be imagined that so many of our Country-men would have opposed us in this quarrel, if they had understood their owne good ; so may we safely promise to ourselves, that when our Common Rights and liberties shall be cleared, their endeavours will be disappointed, that seek to make themselves our Masters : since therefore our former oppressions, and scarce yet ended troubles have beene occasioned, either by want of frequent Nationall meetings in Councell, or by rendring those meetings ineffectuall ; We are fully agreed and resolved, to provide that hereafter our Representatives be neither left to an uncertainty for the time, nor made useless to the ends for which they are intended ; In order whereunto we declare,

I.

That the People of England being at this day very unequally distributed by Counties, Cities and Borroughs, for the election of their Deputies in Parliament, ought to be more indifferently proportioned, according to the number of the Inhabitants : the circumstances whereof, for number, place, and manner, are to be set down before the end of this present Parliament.

II.

That to prevent the many inconveniences apparently arising, from the long continuance of the same persons in authority, this present Parliament be dissolved upon the last day of September, which shall be in the year of our Lord, 1648.

III.

That the People do of course chuse themselves a Parliament once in two yeares, viz. upon the first Thursday in every 2nd. March, after the manner as shall be prescribed before the end of this Parliament, to begin to sit upon the first Thursday in Aprill following at Westminster, or such other place as shall bee appointed from time to time by the preceding Representatives ; and to continue till the last day of September, then next ensuing and no longer.

IV.

That the power of this, and all future Representatives of this Nation, is inferiour only to theirs who chuse them, and doth extend, without the consent or concurrence of any other person or persons ; to the enacting, altering, and repealing of Lawes ; to the erecting and abolishing of Offices and Courts ; to the appointing, removing, and calling to account Magistrates, and Officers of all degrees ; to the making War and peace, to the treating with forraigne States; And generally, to whatsoever is not expresly, or implyedly reserved by the represented to themselves.

Which are as followeth,

1.   That matters of Religion, and the wayes of Gods Worship, are not at all intrusted by us to any humane power, because therein wee cannot remit or exceed a tittle of what our Consciences dictate to be the mind of God, without wilfull sinne : neverthelesse the publike way of instructing the Nation (so it be not compulsive) is referred to their discretion.

2.   That the matter of impresting and constraining any of us to serve in the warres, is against our freedome ;   and therefore we do not allow it in our Representatives ; the rather because money (the sinews of war) being alwayes at their disposall, they can never want numbers of men, apt enough to engage in any just cause.

3. That after the dissolution of this present Parliament, no person be at any time questioned for anything said or done, in reference to the late publike differences, otherwise then in execution of the Judgments of the present Representatives, of House of Commons.

4. That in all Laws made, or to be made, every person may be bound alike, and that no Tenure, Estate, Charter, Degree, Birth, or place, do confer any exemption from the ordinary Course of Legall proceedings, whereunto others are subjected.

5. That as the Laws ought to be equall, so they must be good, and not evidently destructive to the safety and well-being of the people.

These things we declare to be our native Rights, *and therefore are agreed and resolved to maintain them with our utmost possibilities, against all opposition whatsoever, being compelled thereunto, not only by the examples of our Ancestors, whose bloud was often spent in vain for the recovery of their Freedomes, suffering themselves,* through fradulent accommodations, *to be still deluded of the fruit of their Victories, but also by our own wofull experience, who having long expected, & dearly earned the establishment of these certain rules of Government are yet made to depend for the settlement of our Peace and Freedome, upon him that intended our bondage, and brought a cruell Warre upon us.*

Source: British Library, Thomason Tracts E412 (21)

The above transcript of the original on sale in London on the 3rd November 1647 retains the original spelling, capitalization and italicization in order to illustrate those aspects which the authors wished to emphasise.

Appendix II

A FULL RELATION OF

The Proceedings at the Rendezvous of that Brigade of the Army that was held in *Corkbush* field in *Hartford* Parish on Monday last

Nov. 15. 1647   *Imprimatur*   Gilbert Mabbot.

SIR

This day (according to appointment) the Rendezvouz of the first Brigade of the Army was held in Corkbush field in Hartford Parish, between Hartford and Ware. Hartford being the Headquarters Saturday and Sonday, the General went from thence to the Rendezvouz where according to order there met, of Horse : the General's regiment, Col. *Fleetwoods*, Col. *Riches* and Col. *Twistletons;* of Foot, The General's, Col. *Hammonds* and Col. *Prides*; And besides these, upon the seducements of the new Agents, Col. *Harrisons* and Col. *Lilburns* Regiments. The General expressed himself very gallantly and faithfully at the Head of every Regiment, to live and dye with them for those particulars which were contained in a Remonstrance read to every Regiment: And notwithstanding the endeavours of Major *Scot* and others ; to animate the Soldiers to stand to the Paper called *The Agreement of the People*, they generally by many acclamations declared their Affections and Resolutions to adhere to the General; and as many as could in the short time they had allowed, signed an Agreement drawn up for that purpose, concerning their being ready from time to time to observe such Orders as they should receive from the General and Councel of the Army. I had sent you the copy of this Agreement and his Excellencies Remonstrance, but that I was so straitned in time, I could not.

I should have acquainted you before that upon the Generals coming into the field, Col *Eyres*, Major *Scot* and others, were observed to be insinuating divers seditious Principles into the Soldiers, and incensing them against the General and General Officers. Upon which, Order was given for the Commitment of Col. *Eyre* and others into the Marshal's hands; and Major *Scot* committed to

A FULL
RELATION

13

OF

The Proceedings at the Rendezvouz of
that Brigade of the Army that was held in *Corkbush*
field in *Hartford* Parish on Monday laſt.

AND

A LETTER from the Speaker of the Honorable
Houſe of Commons to Sir *Thomas Fairfax*, concerning the ſaid Rendezvouz.

With a PAPER, Entituled,

Englands Freedoms, and Soldiers Rights.

ALSO

A Petition to his Excellency Sir *Thomas Fairfax*, of
divers Officers and Soldiers of the Army
under his Command.

Together with a Declaration againſt the Proceedings
of the new Agents.

---

*Nov.*15.1647.   *Imprimatur*
                    Gilbert Mabbot.

London, Printed for *Laurence Chapman*,
November 16. 1647.

the custody of Lieutenant *Chillenden* and sent up to the Parliament. Some inferior persons were likewise committed for dispensing sundry scandalous and factious Papers, as *The Agreement of the People,* etc. among the private soldiers : And finding that those persons who pretend most for the Freedom of the People had dispersed divers of those Papers amongst Col. *Lilburns* Regiment of Foot (the most mutinous Regiment in the Army) strict Command was given for them to tear them and cast them away ; which was done and Captain-Lieut. *Bray* (who was the onely Officer above a Lieutenant left among them, the rest being driven away by the mutinous Soldiers, and one of them wounded) was taken from the Head of that Regiment and committed to custody; it being alleaged that he had led on the Soldiers to that Rendezvouz contrary to Orders. And afterwards a Councel of War being called in the field, divers Mutiniers for example sake were drawn forth, three of them were tryed and condemned to death, and one of them (whose turn it fell to by lot) was shot to death at the Head of the Regiment, and others are in hold to be tryed.

The Soldiers of this Regiment crying out, that they were abused by their Officers, and being told by the Lieutenant-General, that they should have justice against them, were very much satisfied, sensible of their error, and promised conformity to the General's Commands for the future. Col. *Rainsborough* and some others presented this enclosed petition and *The Agreement of the People* to His Excellency at his first coming : Col. *Harrisons* Regiment, who had them in their Hats with this Motto on the outside in capital Letters, *Englands Freeedoms, and Soldiers Rights*, when they understood their error, tore them out of their Hats, and expressed their Resolution to be obedient to his Excellencies commands. Lieut. Col. *John Lilburn* came this day to Ware : but things not succeeding at the Rendezvouz according to expectation, came not further.

Sir, I cannot but rejoyce in this days Unity, in relation to the Peace of the Kingdom ; so, I hope, That the issue will tend to the benefit thereof ; and that the General and Officers of the Army will do as much for the real freedom of the People, as the others do pretend ; and how good soever their intentions may be, nothing but confusion at present appears in their endeavours. In much haste I rest,

Your affectionate Friend and Servant,

Hartford, 15 *November* 1647   William Clark

Source: British Library, Thomason Tracts E414 (13)

Appendix III

To the Right Honourable *Edward* Earl of *Manchester*, Speaker of the House of Peers *pro Tempore*

My Lord,

I rendezvoused this day three regiments of foot and four of horse, *videlicet*, of horse my own regiment, Colonel *Riche's*, Colonel *Fleetwood's*, and Colonel *Twistleton's*; and of foot, my own regiment, Colonel *Pride's* and Colonel *Hammond's*. When they appeared all at the rendezvous, I tendered to them, and had read in the head of every regiment, this inclosed paper, which was very acceptable to them, and to which they have given very full and clear concurrence, professing readiness to serve you and the kingdom; which I hope will be constantly and honestly by them performed. And I cannot but attribute great acknowledgement to ALMIGHTY GOD, in making these poor men so unanimous in such things as I think do and will conduce to an happy settlement of this poor kingdom : They profess likewise an absolute submission and conformity to the ancient discipline of the Army, by which I hope to order it to your satisfaction. There came thither also two regiments without orders ; *videlicet*, Colonel *Harrison's* of horse and Colonel *Lilburne's* of foot. These two had been very much abused and deluded by the Agents who had their intercourses at London, and were so far prevailed withal, that when they came into the field, they brought with them in their hats a paper, commonly called *"The Agreement of the People"*, being very much inflamed towards mutiny and disobedience : But truly perceived the men were merely cozened and abused with fair pretences of those men that acted in the *London* counsels. For Colonel *Harrison's* regiment, they were no sooner informed of their error, but with a great deal of readiness and chearfulness, they submitted to me, expressing the same affection and resolution of obedience with other regiments ; and I do believe you will have a very good account of them for time to come. As for Colonel *Lilburne's*, they were put into those extremities of discontent, that they had driven away almost all their officers, and came in marching up near to the rendezvous, contrary to orders ; the chiefest officer with them being a Captain-Lieutenant, whom I have secured, on purpose to try him at a Council of War ; and for example sake drew out divers of the mutineers, three whereof were presently tried and condemned to death, and by lot, one of them was shot to death in the head of the regiment ; and there are more in hold to be tried. I do find the same regiment likewise very sensible of their error, and testifying much seeming conformity to commands ; so that I doubt not but I shall be able to give you a good account of that regiment also

And indeed I do see that the *London* Agents have been the great authors of these irregularities, and with some of better quality have not been their abettors.

Major *Scott* came to the rendezvous and did carry himself very factiously; not only testifying his own discontent, but stirring up others also to the same; whereupon I desired him to withdraw out of the field, and to repair to the Parliament ; and commanded an officer to attend him to the House of Commons.

I thought it my duty to give your Lordships this further account, That Colonel *Rainborow* with some others tended this inclosed petition, together with the *People's Agreement* annexed thereunto ; and by what hands I yet know not fully, very many copies of the same Agreement were dispersed amongst the soldiers, thereby to engage them ; but blessed be GOD! all proved ineffectual.

And I may repeat it once again, that I never yet, upon any Rendezvous, found men better composed and better satisfied at parting than those nine regiments were ; and I trust in GOD, if a just care be taken to answer their reasonable desires, they will so continue. But give me leave to say, I hope out of a good affection to you and this poor kingdom, That it will be your Lordship's glory and honour, to make such use of this Mercy, as that all the world may see, that which I know you intend ; to wit a speedy settlement of those things I was bold to present in my late addresses to the House of Commons ; and the easing of this poor kingdom from Free Quarter, by providing future pay, that so no free quarter may be taken, nor the soldiers put to shifts, nor I made unable to uphold the Discipline of the Army ; that they may be satisfied in their arrears, according to former desires ; and the Act of Indemnity made full ; and those other things concerning the soldiers in this paper performed. I shall very much rejoice in the next place, that you will be pleased to anticipate all our desires, in those things which concern the settlement of the Kingdom ; which though they do not move so properly from us, as soldiers, yet as *Englishmen*, who have engaged ourselves by our several declarations to the kingdom, we cannot but continue our humble and earnest desires, that they may be settled to satisfaction ; and we hope it will not be any regret to you, that we became your Remembrancers therein.

And my Lords, believe me, you will find Expedition will be the life of all, in the things which concern the soldiers of this kingdom.   We shall have our other rendezvous with what conveniency may be ; of the issue of which, you shall receive a speedy account.   There be four regiments of horse : one in Wales *videlicet* Colonel *Huton's* ;   Colonel *Scroope's* in *Som'settsheire* ;   Colonel *Tomlinson's* in *Lincolnesheir* ;   Colonel *Thorney's* in *Nottinghamsheir* ;   of which I have very good assurances they will be very faithful and obedient to you and the Discipline of the Army.   Having troubled you thus much, I rest your Lordship's

Most Humble Servant

T Fairfax

Hartford 15° Novembris 1647

Source: Journal of the House of Lords Volume 9 (1646-7) pp 527-8

Appendix IV

The Humble Petition to Fairfax

To his Excellency, Sir *Thomas Fairefax* our Noble General. The humble petition of many Officers and Soldiers under his command.

Sheweth,

That, in judgement and conscience, we engaged in the war against the king, under your Excellency's command, to preserve and vindicate the Freedoms of our native country, and of the Parliament in order thereunto.

That by the blessing of GOD, all those our enemies are fallen or fled before us.

That, for the same ends, and for our own rights for our service, we were forced to hazard ourselves in disputing the Parliament's commands; and those our opposers have been likewise subdued.

That the countries have petitioned your Excellency to procure the long-expected settlement of their freedoms.

That we have waited many months, for the securing to us and all the freeborn people their native rights, and for our indemnity and arrears as soldiers; and our hearts bleed, to see our Country consume under continued distractions and heavy oppressions.

That we see no hope of indemnity for us and our assistants, nor of settling the Foundations of Freedom, but by entering into this Agreement; which we herewith offer to your Excellency, desiring your concurrence therein.

That we have seen and felt the sad consequences of being divided and scattered, before our native freedoms were settled, and our arrears secured, and such a way established for constant pay, that we may know where to receive it monthly without fail.

That we are bound in conscience, from the sense of our duty to our native country, and in mercy to ourselves, to keep together, with our swords in our hands, to maintain these our freedoms, for which the Parliament first invited us to take arms, to see our arrears and pay secured, and our dear country freed from its intolerable burthens.

May it therefore please your excellency, to go on in owning and leading us, in maintenance of this our cause, to the righteousness whereof GOD hath borne such clear witnes. And in the prosecution of these things, we humbly desire to live and die under your Excellency's conduct.

The *People's Ingagement* was annexed to this Petition, with these words printed on the back side in great letters. ENGLAND's FREEDOM, SOLDIERS RIGHTS

Source: Journal of the House of Lords Volume 9 (1646-7) page 528
also reproduced in British Library, Thomason Tracts E412 (13)

Appendix V

Remonstrance to the Soldiers

A Remonstrance from his Excellency, Sir *Thomas Fairefax*, and his Council of War, concerning the late discontent and distraction in the Army ; with his Excellency's Declaration of himself, and expectation from the Army thereupon, and for the future uniting the Army.

That ever since the Engagement of the Army at *Newmarket Heath*, his Excellency, with the General Officers and General Council of the Army (to which that Engagement refers) have been doing their Duty and best endeavour for the good of the Army and kingdom, according to the ends of that engagement and the declarations and other papers that have since passed from the Army.

And in this (according to their consciences and the best of their understandings), they have done the utmost they could, without present destruction to the Parliament, which in their opinions would inevitably have put the kingdom into blood and confusion, and so both the army and kingdom into an incapacity, or past all rational hopes, of attaining or enjoying that satisfaction or security for which the engagement was entered into ; and if they have neglected any thing wherein they might have done better, they have been ready (as still they are) to be convinced thereof, and to amend the default, and to hearken to what any man would soberly offer for that purpose, or to lead them to any thing better.

That while they have been thus doing their duty (besides many other interruptions or diversion by the designs and workings of enemies), they have of late found the greatest interruptions to their proceedings by a few men, members of the army, who (without any authority, or just call there unto, that we know of, assuming the name of agents for several regiments) have (for what ends we know not) taken upon them to act as a divided party from the said Council and Army, and associating themselves with, or rather (as we have just cause to believe) give themselves up to be acted or guided by, divers private persons that are not of the army, have endeavoured, by various falsehoods and scandals, raised and divulged in print, and otherwise, against the General, the General Officers and Council, to possess the Army and kingdom with jealousies of them, and prejudices against them (as if they were fallen from their

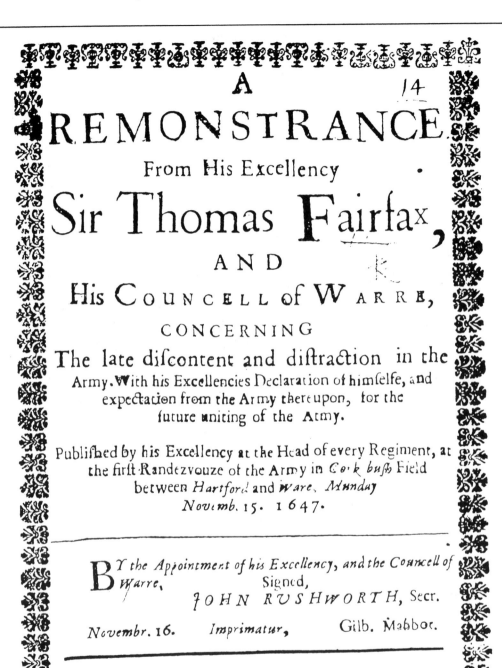

A

14

REMONSTRANCE,

From His Excellency

Sir Thomas Fairfax,

AND

His COUNCELL of WARRE,

CONCERNING

The late difcontent and diftraction in the
Army. With his Excellencies Declaration of himfelfe, and
expectation from the Army thereupon, for the
future uniting of the Army.

Publifhed by his Excellency at the Head of every Regiment, at
the firft Randezvouze of the Army in *Cork bufh* Field
between *Hartford* and *Ware*, *Munday*
Novemb. 15. 1647.

BY the *Appointment of his Excellency, and the Councell of*
Warre, Signed,
JOHN RUSHWORTH, Secr.

Novembr. 16. *Imprimatur,* Gilb. Mabbot.

London, Printed for *George Whittington*, at the Blew Anchor
in Cornhill neere the Royall Exchange, 1647.

principles, had broke all their engagements and declarations, and thereby forfeited their trust, and were in their whole proceedings false and treacherous both to the Army and kingdoms).

And by these and other practices, the said Agents and their associates have laboured to make parties and factions in the Army, to raise discontents, mutinies and disorders therein, to divide the soldiers from the officers, and both officers and soldiers amongst themselves, and to withdraw several parts of the army from their duty and obedience to the General's orders, (and that) in things most necessary for the safety of the Army and kingdom.

And thus while they causelessly cry out against breach of engagements and dividing the army, they themselves have made, or endeavoured to make, the greatest breaches of their engagements and greatest dividing of the Army that can be ; a dividing most truly contrary to their engagements, a dividing which is as bad and destructive as disbanding, even the dissolution of all that order, combination and government, which is the essence of an army ; and under false and delusive pretences (that the engagements have been broken), they have endeavoured really to loosen and draw the army off from its former engagements, and to draw it into new engagements, different from, and (in some things) destructive to, the former ; and have thus endangered the greatest forfeiture of the Faith, and Honour of the Army that ever it incurred.

And whilst they cry out there is nothing done, they themselves have made the greatest obstructions to the doing of any good for the Army or Kingdom, both in the hindrance and delays to our proceedings and the expence of time which with their workings have occasioned (either to have satisfied them (if it had been possible) or else to salve and quiet those discontents and distractions which they have raised in the Army) ; and also by the occasions which the Parliament and kingdom (yea even our best friends in both) have thus received to discourage them from compliance with, or confidence in, an army so uncertain, so unsettled, so divided.

For these causes, the General hath thought fit to rendezvous the army or such parts of it as are not fixed upon necessary duty elsewhere ; and having (with the advice of the General Council) sent to the Parliament more importunately than before for speedy satisfaction to the army in their just desires (especially in point of provision for constant pay to avoid free quarter, and of security for arrears), thought it best (with the same advice) to dismiss most of the officers and agitators from the Head Quarters, for a fortnight, unto their respective regiments, to satisfy and compose these discontents and division which have thus been raised in them ; and for ease of the country, and accommodation to the soldiery (with respect to the season of the year), thought fit to contract the quarters of the army in three brigades, and to draw them to three several Rendezvous not far from each other, and this in order to one general rendezvous, if there should be any occasion ; and in this the several regiments of horse and foot have been appointed to contract quarters, in order to those several rendezvous, by taking them directly in order as their several quarters lay before, without any other respect or consideration.

But even these things the said pretended agents and their associates have laboured to pervert and make advantage of, to the aforesaid ends of discontent and distraction and to represent the same to the several regiments as done in pursuance of the same treacherous counsels and designs which they had before suggested :

And what good they could not deny to be in the things, they assume to themselves as gained by their procurement ; and so greedily catch at the sole credit of it, as if the General and his Council (but for them) had not done it ; and by letters and messages contradicting the General's order, they have (under such scandalous pretences) laboured to draw divers regiments from their quarters and rendezvous to which they were ordered, unto the first rendezvous near *Ware*, in a disorderly and confused manner to the oppression of the country, and disaccommodation (if not quarrelling and distraction) of the soldiery in quartering.

That without redress of these abuses and disorders, his Excellency cannot nor will any longer undergo or undertake further to discharge his present trust to the Parliament, and the Army and Kingdom.

That though he is far above any such low thoughts as to court or woo the Army to continue him their General ; yet to discharge himself to the utmost, and bring the business to a clear and certain issue, his Excellency doth now declare:

"That he is yet willing to adhere to, and to conduct, and live and die with the army in the lawful prosecution of these things following : *(videlicet)*

First for the soldiery to obtain:

1. Present provision for constant pay while continued ; to enable them to discharge quarters.

2.   The present stating of accompts and security of arrears ; with an effectual and speedy course to raise monies thereupon.

3.   Sufficient indemnity, and Commissioners in every County for that purpose.

4.   Provision for maimed soldiers, and the widows and orphans of men slain in the service (and that in a certain and more honourable way) ; with Commissioners in every county for that purpose.

5.   Provisions for freedom from pressing, according to the first petition of the army.

6. Provision for freedom of apprentices that have served in this war, with a penalty upon masters refusing to give it.

Secondly for the kingdom:

A period to be set to this present Parliament (to end so soon as may be with safety) and Provision therewith to be made for future parliaments ; for the certainty of their meeting, sitting & ending ; and for the freedom and equality of elections thereto ; to render the House of Commons (as near as may be) an equal representative of the people that are to elect.

And (according to the Representation of the Army, of June the 14th) to leave other things to, and acquiesce in the determinations of, Parliament ; but to mind the Parliament of, and mediate with them for, redress of the common grievances of the people, and all other things that the army have declared their desires for.

That upon his Excellency's continued conjunction in these things, he expects that, for the particular circumstances of them, the army shall (according to their aforesaid first engagements) acquiesce in what shall be agreed unto by the General Council of the Army to which that engagement refers ; and for matter of ordering, conduct, and Government of the Army, that every member of it shall be observant of, and subject to, his Excellency, his Council of War, and every one of his superior officers, according to the discipline of war ; for assurance whereof, he expects that as many as are satisfied herewith, and agree hereunto, do severally subscribe to what is hereunder written for that purpose.

We, the officers and soldiers of . . . .
. . . . . Regiment of . . . . , whose names are here subscribed, do hereby declare, that we are satisfied in his Excellency the General's continued Conjunction with the army, in the lawful prosecution of the things here before declared to be prosecuted for the soldiery and kingdom respectively; and for the particular circumstances of them, we shall (according to the general engagement of the army above-mentioned) acquiesce in what shall be agreed unto by the General Council of the Army to which that Engagement refers : And for the matter of ordering, conduct and government of the army, we shall be observant of, and subject to, his Excellency, his Council of War, and every one of us to our superior officers in this Regiment and the Army, according to the Discipline of War.

Hertford 14 November 1647

Signed by the appointment of his Excellency Sir *Thomas Fairefax* and the Council of War

Jo. Rushworth, Secretary.

Source: Journal of the House of Lords Volume 9 (1646-7) pp 529-31
also reproduced in British Library, Thomason Tracts E414 (14)

Appendix VI

Extracts from Parliamentary Newspapers
November 1647

The Kingdom's Weekly Intelligencer No 234, 9-16 November 1647

Thursday November 11

"It was this day certified from the Army that there should be a generall Rendezvous on the Monday following at Ware, on Tuesday at St. Albans & on Wednesday at Kingston, at which time the sense of the Army will be known and a unanimous establishment indeavoured for the safety of the Kingdome, and the satisfaction of the Souldier."

Monday November 15

"Collonell *Rainsborough* informed the House what danger might ensue upon the Rendezvous there being no money ready to pay the souldiers, the House had thereupon a debate upon the deferring of the Rendezvous, but it could not conveniently be done in regard the souldiers were upon their march to the Rendezvous, which is to continue this day, *Tuesday* and *Wednesday*.

There was a Report delivered with confidence, that his Majesty would appeare today at the Rendezvous at *Ware*, but that expectation was frustrated for by letters this day from Lieutenant General *Hammond*, the Governour of the Isle of *Wight*, it was certified his Majesty had ventured his Person by sea to the Isle of *Wight*. "

Source: British Library, Thomason Tracts, E416 (1)

The Moderate Intelligencer No 139, 11-18 November 1647

"The 13th They (the Commons) considered of money for the Army, which *Monday* and *Tuesday* was in part expected at *Ware* ; some thought there would be 15 Regiments there, the General, passing by *London* this afternoon to go to the place aforesaid, also Lieut.-General and Commissary-General."

"The 16th From the Headquarters it is certified thus much, that the Gen. declaration did most import the assumption of Discipline, that Col. Harrison's regiment was drawn to the headquarters by the perswasion of one Allin of that Regiment, who told them that he had found out as much mony of a malignant, as would pay the Army for three moneths, and that his Excellency had made choice of that Regiment to secure it, a most rational argument. The papers in the Hats of the soldiers when the Gen. exprest his dislike, were all pulled out. One Ayres, a Lieut. Colonell was committed for offering to divide the Army: The foot, before the Declaration muttered about the King, but no signall being given, it did not appear whether pro or contra.

The Gen. was very vigorous to bring the Army into order, who God knows had no hand in disordering it, and now for a sudden agreement, or settlement that there be no more use of Agitators, and that they may continue as other men."

Source: British Library, Thomason Tracts, E416 (8)

Perfect Occurrences No.46, 12—19 November 1647

Tuesday November 16th

"Both Houses received papers from the Army of a good agreement at a Randezvouzes neer *Ware* the day before, accusing divers Citizens to labour to have made factions and discords.   Major Scot a member of the House committed. Col. Rainsborough taxed about Petitions. 2 regiments that came with papers perswaded to comply.   3 souldiers who had mutinied the Fryday before about Dunstable (where 2 were killed and a Lieutenant's hand cut off) cast lots for their lives and 2 shot the 3° to death"

Source: British Library, Thomason Tracts, E520 (6)

A Perfect Diurnal No. 225, 15—22 November 1647

18 November

"Of the two later Randezvouz yesterday and this day we heard by letters this accompt

Our business yesterday was quickly over there being at the second Randezvouz upon Ruislip Heath but three troopes of Col. *Okey's* Dragoons and two Regiments of foot viz. Sir *Hardress Waller's* and Col. *Lambert's* : but as our work was short (so I hope) are .. There being no other expressions, but of continued concurrence with and submission to the General.

Thursday Nov. 18. The third Randezvouz of the Army was upon the Hain Warren neer Kingston : There were present according to orders : the Lieut. Generalls, Com. *Iretons*, and Col. *Whallies*, Regiment of horse, Col. *Rainsborows*, Col. *Barkesteads*, Col. *Overtons* and Col. *Hewsons*, of foot and The Generall's life guard. There appeared no thing of discontent, or dismision but a ready agreement to his Excellencies Remonstrance, and subjection to his Excellencies commands."

Source: British Library, Thomason Tracts, E520 (7)

The Kingdom's Weekly Intelligencer No 235, 16—23 November 1647

"Three souldiers that had made a Mutinie three days before (in which two were killed and a Lieutenant's hand cut off) did cast lotts for their lives, and the two, whom the lott reprieved, did shoot the third to death."

Source: British Library, Thomason Tracts, E416 (28)

Appendix VII

Letter from the House of Lords
to General Fairfax

Thanks for "The seasonable suppressing of those mutinous persons, whose factious designs might probably have destroyed the good discipline of the army and likewise endangered the safety of the Parliament with a hazard of the subversion of the fundamental government of this kingdom. They are well pleased that some justice hath been done upon those that appeared in opposition to you; and they desire you still to continue your care, to the further execution of exemplary punishment upon those who have, or shall endeavour to raise mutinie, and factiously to subvert the orderly regulation of the army — "

Source: Journal of the House of Lords Volume 9 (1646-7) p 536
20 November 47

Bibliography

Manuscript Sources

Public Record Office:

Records of the Parliamentary committee for taking the accounts of the Kingdom (SP 28) Volumes relating to Hertfordshire:
Volume 154 Account Book of William Turner, Treasurer 1647 ff 8-12
Volume 233 Unfoliated and unnumbered bundle — Hertfordshire Committee Expenses and Receipts of William Turner, Treasurer

State Papers Domestic Interregnum (SP 46) Volume 97 ff 71A r & 71A v, Colonel Reynolds' letter to Cromwell re. Lieutenant Rockwell; f 77B, Rockwell's confession re. the Ware Mutiny.

Bodleian Library:

Tanner Ms 58 (on microfilm in Institute of Historical Research, London University)
f 159, A Letter from a Commissioner with the Army at St. Albans to Parliament (3 June 1647)
f 435, Draft letter from Speaker Lenthall to the Committee of Hertford (31 July 1647)

Hertfordshire Record Office:

D/Ex 67 P 1, Map showing Cockbush Field

St. Albans City Muniments:

Mayor's Accounts for 1647

Printed Primary Sources

(BL = British Library, Thomason Tracts)

Anon, *A copy of a letter sent by the Agents of severall Regiments* (11 November 1647), *BL, E413 (18)*

Anon, *A copy of a letter sent to his excellency* (1647) *BL, E413 (17)*

Anon, *A New Declaration* (25 November 1647) *BL, E416 (35)*

Anon, *A Preparation for a day of Thanksgiving* (1647) *BL, E402 (31)*

Anon, *Four petitions from four counties to Fairfax* (1647) *BL, E393 (7)*

Anon, *His Majesties most Gracious Declaration* (11 November 1647) *BL, E413 (15)*

Anon, *Last newes from the Armie* (1647) *BL, E393 (14)*

Anon, *The Machivilian Cromwellist* (10 January 1648) *BL, E422 (12)*

Anon, *Newes from the Army* (1647) *BL, E392 (23)*

Anon, *Petition from Hertfordshire and Buckinghamshire* (1647) *BL, 669 f10 (115)*

Anon, *The Humble Petition of Divers Well-affected inhabitants of Oxon., Bucks., and Herts.* (14 September 1647) *BL, E407 (29)*

Anon, *The Humble Remonstrance and desires of divers officers and soldiers in the army under the command of Colonel Hewson* (9 November 1647) *BL, E413 (6)*

Anon, *The justice of the army against evil doers vindicated* (5 June 1649) — includes Bray's Narrative *BL, E558 (14)*

Anon, *Two petitions to the General's Excellency* (1 November 1647) *BL, E412 (18)*

Bell, R. (ed) *Memorials of the Civil War. The Fairfax Correspondence,* Vol. I (1849)

Bray, W. *A Letter to his Excellency Sir Thomas Fairfax from Captaine Lieutenant Bray* (3 January 1648) *BL, E421 (27)*

Bray, W. *A Representation to the Nation BL, E422 (27)*

Burch, W., *Letter from Redborne* (15 June 1647) *BL, E393 (4)*

Carlyle, T. *Oliver Cromwell's Letters and Speeches* (5 Vols. London, 1887)

Clarke, William *A Letter from his Excellency Sir Thomas Fairfax to Mr Speaker concerning a Randezvous of the Army* (8 November 1647) *BL, E413 (19)*

Clarke, William *A full relation of the Proceedings at the Rendezvous,* 15 November 1647, *BL, E414 (13)*

Firth C.H. (ed.) *The Clarke Papers* (New Edition, Royal Historical Society, 1992)

Firth C.H. (ed.) *Memoirs of Edmund Ludlow,* 2 Vols (Oxford, 1894)

Haller W. and Davies G. *The Leveller Tracts 1647-1653* (Columbia UP, 1944)

Hill C. and Dell E. *The Good Old Cause: the English Revolution of 1640-1660* (2nd Ed. 1969)

Kingdom's Weekly Intelligencer, Nos. 227, 234, 235, 239 *BL, E407 (35); E416 (1 & 28); E421 (3)*

Lilburne, John and Overton, Richard *The outcryes of Oppressed Commons BL, E378 (13)*

Maseres F. (ed.) "Memoirs of Denzil Lord Holles", in *Select Tracts Relating to the Civil wars in England* (2 Vols. 1699)

Mercurius Elenctius No. 45 *BL, E414 (4)*

Mercurius Melancholicus No. 11 *BL, E414 (11)*

Moderate Intelligencer Nos. 138, 139 *BL E414 (1); E416 (8)*

Morton A.L. *Freedom in Arms — A Selection of Leveller Writings* (London, 1975)

Perfect Diurnall, Nos. 210, 224, 225, 227-31 *BL E520 (5, 7, 11, 14, 17, 19, 21)*

Perfect Occurrences, Nos. 44, 45, 46, 48, 50, 51, 52 *BL, E518 (16); E520 (2, 4, 6, 10, 16, 18, 20)*

Perfect Weekly Account, Nos. 43, 46, 47, 48 *BL E412 (17); E416 (2, 27); E419 (17)*

Prince, T., Chidley, S., et al, *The Humble Petition of many freeborn people* (1647) *BL, 669 f11 (89)*

Rushworth J. *Historical Collections of Private Passages of State*, 8 Vols, (London 1721-2) Vol. VII.

The Moderate Intelligencer, No.139, *BL E416 (8)*

Scrope R. and Monkhouse T. (eds.) *State papers collected by Edward Earl of Clarendon, commencing 1621*, 3 Vols. (Oxford 1767-86)

The Journals of the House of Commons, Vol. 5, (1803)

The Journals of the House of Lords, Vol. 9 (n.d.)

Tibbutt, H.G. "The Tower of London Letter Book of Sir Lewis Dyve 1646-47" in *Bedfordshire Records Society Publications*, Vol. XXVII (Luton, 1957)

Whitelock, B. *Memorials of English Affairs* 4 Vols. (Oxford 1853) Vol. 2

Wolfe, D.M. *Leveller Manifestoes of the Puritan Revolution* (London 1944)

Secondary Sources

Aylmer, G.E. *The Levellers in the English Revolution*, (London, 1975)

Brailsford, H.N. *The Levellers and the English Revolution* (1976)

Capp, B.S. *The Fifth Monarchy Men — A study in seventeenth century Millenarianism*, (London, 1972)

Coward B. *Oliver Cromwell* (London, 1991)

Gentles I. *The New Model Army in England, Ireland and Scotland 1645-1653* (London, 1992)

Greaves R.L. and Zaller, R.E. (eds.), *Biographical Dictionary of British Radicals in the Seventeenth Century*, 3 Vols. (1981-4)

Gregg P. *Free-born John — A Biography of John Lilburne* (London, 1961)

Kishlansky M. *What happened at Ware?* Historical Journal, 25, (1982) pp 827-39

Morrill J. *The Nature of the English Revolution* (London, 1993)

Ogle, O & Bliss B.C.L. (eds.)*Calendar of the Clarendon State Papers*, Vol. I (Oxford, 1872)

Shaw H. *The Levellers* (London, 1968)

Underdown D. "Honest Radicals in the counties 1642-9", in Pennington D.H. & Thomas, K. (eds.) *Puritans and Revolutionaries. Essays in seventeenth century history presented to Christopher Hill* (Oxford, 1978), pp 195-204

Woodhouse A.S.P. *Puritanism and Liberty* (2nd Ed, Chicago, 1974)

Woolrych A. "Putney revisited, Political debate in the New Model Army in 1647" in Jones C. et al (eds.) *Politics and People in Revolutionary England. Essays in honour of Ivan Roots* (Oxford 1986), pp 95-116.

Woolrych A. *Soldiers and Statesmen: The General Council of the Army and its Debates 1647-1648* (Clarendon Press, Oxford, 1987)

Index

(Page numbers in bold italics indicate illustrations)